To Alex
Bill a
Smooth

Happy Jubilee

MAWU

7-8-14

Praise for *Magic in a Shaker* . . .

"This book will inspire everyone to enjoy a creative cocktail for any occasion with friends, family, or anyone you meet at your favorite watering hole. Marvin has given information for not only those in the cocktail business but the person who wants to learn what a great cocktail is all about and how to make it."
—Bernie Ralston, president, L'Esprit du Bon Vin

"Bartender Marvin J. Allen quickly earned our nickname 'Marvelous Marvin' as we watched him perform day in and day out. Creating *marvelous* cocktails from nothing more than flavor-profile suggestions brought constant raves of approval from the guests; then, for the 'garnish' to the total cocktail experience, Marvin shared stories about New Orleans and histories of ingredients, much to the appreciation of those around the historic Carousel Bar. Marvin's warm, entertaining personality, along with his amazing knowledge of all things cocktail . . . makes 'Marvelous' a destination bartender from all four corners of the earth . . . he truly is a 'Marvelous' Michelangelo of Mixology!"
—J. Kevin Jenkins, host/creator, *Chef and the Fatman Radio Show*

"The Carousel Bar is a time-honored tradition, revered by locals and visitors alike as the perfect place to celebrate life in the Big Easy. Located in the Hotel Monteleone, the Carousel Bar has been spinning for sixty-five years. If you are lucky enough to grab a coveted barstool, during each fifteen-minute rotation is the time to meet Marvin Allen, celebrated bartender and adopted New Orleanian. Marvin personifies magic in a shaker. Just tell him what you like to drink, and he will create a customized cocktail while sharing historical happenings at the Carousel and entertaining you with spirited tales and tidbits. And when you've downed your last drink, you will have experienced one of the most delightful traditions New Orleans has to offer, made memorable by bartender extraordinaire, Marvin Allen."

—Betsie Gambel, president, Gambel Communications

MAGIC
IN A SHAKER

MAGIC
IN A SHAKER

A Year of Spirited Libations

Marvin J. Allen

Photographs by Ann Benoit

PELICAN PUBLISHING COMPANY
GRETNA 2014

The word "Pelican" and the depiction of a pelican are
trademarks of Pelican Publishing Company, Inc., and are
registered in the U.S. Patent and Trademark Office.

Library of Congress Cataloging-in-Publication Data

Allen, Marvin J.
  Magic in a shaker : a year of spirited libations / by Marvin J.
Allen ; photographs by Ann Benoit.
    pages cm
  Includes index.
  ISBN 978-1-4556-1989-4 (hardcover : alk. paper) -- ISBN 978-1-
4556-1990-0 (e-book) 1. Cocktails. 2. Seasonal cooking. I. Title.
  TX951.A363 2014
  641.87′4--dc23

                                    2014011382

Printed in the United States of America
Published by Pelican Publishing Company, Inc.
1000 Burmaster Street, Gretna, Louisiana 70053

CONTENTS

INTRODUCTION

This book is a compilation of my experience as a bartender since the 1990s. It is by no means the absolute authority on the art and magic of mixing cocktails. This book rather is an overview of the different spirits and some of the cocktails that are prepared with them. A lot of my knowledge has come from reading and studying various cocktail and spirits books. I include a list in the back of the book for further reading on the subject. I have written this book in hopes of spiking interest in the magic of mixing cocktails and educating further.

Many people think that mixing cocktails is complicated and requires a lot of knowledge, but I believe just the opposite. Once one has mastered a few basic techniques, the magic of mixing cocktails becomes second nature. And I do consider it magic, not art. You place a few ingredients in either a shaker or glass, then shake or stir, and—voilà—you have a great-tasting beverage. If you use the basic recipe and replace one or two ingredients, you will have created something very different and delicious. Don't be afraid to experiment and create your own magic in a shaker.

I would like to acknowledge and thank the management of the Hotel Monteleone in New Orleans, where I have been employed in the Carousel Bar since 2002, for the support they have given me to practice my magic. Special thanks go out to the late William ("Billy") Monteleone and the Monteleone family for their support and encouragement of my cocktail creations in the bar and for his foresight in having it renovated in 2011. I would also like to acknowledge Ron Pincus, Steve Caputo, Gary Schwartz, and Linda King, who have all been very supportive in this effort.

I would like to thank all my friends at Superior Grill, who put up with me while I wrote on the patio and found inspiration.

I hope you, the reader of this book, will gain some knowledge and the confidence to practice and create some magic in a shaker. Have fun and enjoy.

And remember always to consume responsibly, so you may live to create another day.

MAGIC
IN A SHAKER

CHAPTER 1

THE BEGINNING

DARK AGES OF COCKTAILS

On January 16, 1920, the Dark Ages of Cocktails began, more commonly referred to as Prohibition. This is when as a nation we decided to ban the sale and consumption of alcoholic beverages for our own good. During this period many of the great cocktails and their creators were lost in the United States. The celebrated bartenders of the time either changed careers or left the country to ply their trade. Some went to Europe, others to South America. During this dark period, much of the alcohol that was available was of poor quality. In order to make it more palatable, bartenders would add a lot of sugar syrup, juices, and other masking flavors. Most consumption was done at illegal speakeasies and behind closed doors. The true flavor of the spirit was lost.

Once Prohibition ended on December 5, 1933, it was not until the mid-1980s that we finally began to fully recover. I realize that sounds a little crazy, but if you follow the timeline, it does make sense. When Prohibition ended, we were in the midst of the Great Depression and the Dust Bowl, and cocktails were not of major importance. Then we entered World War II, and almost everyone was involved one way or another. No one was really focusing on pleasure drinking or creating great cocktails.

In the 1950s, Don the Beachcomber Restaurant in California became popular for its tiki cocktails, as we started to consume more for enjoyment. Even though such cocktails are great when made properly with fresh ingredients, bar owners and bartenders soon went the cheap route, using inferior ingredients. Consequently they lost their popularity, but the original recipes are now being rediscovered.

In the 1960s, the martini (vodka) and Manhattans became popular, leading to the three-martini lunch.

In the 1970s, the frozen daiquiri became popular, along with such cocktails as the Long Island iced tea. We also began to discover wine, and wine bars flourished into the 1980s. Again, not much effort was really put into great cocktails, as we still wanted our spirit flavors masked.

Also, a lot of "trashcan punch" was being consumed on college campuses. Each party guest would bring a bottle of spirits and empty it into a large container. A large quantity of fruit juice was added to mask the flavors of the inexpensive alcohol, which was all the students could afford. All this did was get us drunk and give us massive hangovers. It is a wonder any of us survived this era of drinking.

In the mid-1980s, the modern cocktail age was born. People such as Dale DeGroff, Tony Abou-Ganim, David Wondrich, Ted Haigh (a.k.a. Dr. Cocktail), and Gaz Reagan, to name just a few, started to research and recreate the cocktails of old. They resumed using fresh ingredients and premium spirits. When imbibers tasted these classics, they were amazed. The base spirit became the dominant flavor, and mixers became the costars.

Then in 2002 in New Orleans, an event occurred that really jumpstarted the cocktail movement: Tales of the Cocktail. This is held each July, and what started out with about twelve people in the rear of the Carousel Bar in the Hotel Monteleone has grown into one of the city's premier events. It brings together bartenders, distillers, and liquor distributors to showcase their talents and wares and exchange ideas on ways to improve the industry. The event also attracts the home bartender, the curious, and anyone looking to get started in the beverage field.

When all of the above is taken into consideration, you can see why I think that it has been only since the mid-1980s that we have finally shaken off the last vestiges of Prohibition. Let's hope we never have to live through that again.

This book is for the beginner or the superstar who wants to learn a little more or dust off rusty knowledge or techniques. It is written in fairly simple language and hopefully is easy to understand.

Let us begin our journey into the land of spirits and cocktails.

COCKTAILS 101

Anyone can make good cocktails. It is not some closely guarded secret. It is not a skill that takes years of practice or painstaking effort. It can be learned fairly easily and quickly. So why are there so few who can create and make great cocktails? Hopefully the next few pages will help answer that question.

First, people fail to realize the importance of using the finest and freshest ingredients. An old adage says, "A cocktail is only as good as its poorest ingredient." As an example, the difference between a poor martini and a great one is the gin and the vermouth. If you use a superior vermouth but a cheap gin, you will have an inferior martini, with the harsh gin being the predominant flavor. Likewise, if you use a great gin and a poor-quality vermouth, the results will not taste good.

Second, most people fail to understand the basic principles of mixing cocktails. They haphazardly combine a myriad of ingredients, with no fundamental knowledge of how they complement each other. Third, many people fail to follow well-established recipes. They may be lazy or may use inferior or wrong ingredients. An example would be using Rose's lime juice or canned or frozen orange juice as a substitute for fresh squeezed. The garnishes may be old and wilted. All of these factor into producing a great cocktail or a poor one. A bar may be guilty of this if it wants to make as much money as it can and is less concerned about quality. Such bars may think that if they substitute a less expensive item, they will save money, but in the long run, they will lose. The guests will not like the cocktails and send them back, or they will not patronize the establishment any longer. This is especially true if the customer is used to a great-tasting cocktail, orders one, and finds that the bar has lowered the quality of product to save money. Most guests will spend a little more money to have a superior cocktail.

WHAT IS A COCKTAIL?

The definition of a cocktail is a chilled beverage that consists of some or all of the following four ingredients:

Spirits
Bitters
Flavoring
Sweetener

Most cocktails will not have all of these, but you need to assess how the ingredients you do use play with each other in the cocktail. A well-made cocktail . . .

should stimulate the appetite, not dull it. In other words, the cocktail is pleasing to the palate and dances on and tingles the taste buds. It should not be overly bitter, sweet, or dry but well balanced.

should be capable of stimulating the mind. The sharing of cocktails aids in romance, deepens friendships, and helps in other social interactions, to name a few benefits.

should be pleasing to the eye. The garnishes must be fresh and full of color. Remember that a lot of taste comes from sight. If something appears fresh, pleasing, and appetizing, it generally will taste great. Likewise, if you use dull and stale garnishes, no matter how wonderful the cocktail would have tasted, its appearance will diminish its flavor and, more importantly, indicate that you do not care.

should have enough of the base spirit to be readily distinguishable from the other ingredients but not so overpowering that it overshadows the rest of the ingredients.

should be well iced, or in the case of martinis, Manhattans, or other cocktails that are served "up," well chilled.

When and only when you have mastered the above five principles of cocktail mixing will they become second nature to you. You can then have the confidence to experiment with creating variations of classics or your own special cocktail.

Every well-made cocktail needs at least two ingredients to be properly called a cocktail: the base spirit and a modifying agent such as an aromatic, fruit juice, or smoothing agent. In some cases flavoring or coloring agents may be added.

The base is the fundamental and most distinguishable ingredient. It usually makes up at least 25 percent of the cocktail's volume. The base is a spirit such as whiskey, rum, vodka, etc. These liquors are at least 80 proof. Mixing two or more liquors, while not forbidden, is not generally done. Be very careful if you do so, or you may create something very unpleasing to the palate.

The modifying agent is bit more difficult to describe. It adds a layer of flavor to the base spirit but does not drown it out. As examples, think how chocolate syrup enhances the flavor of vanilla ice cream or how catsup enhances the flavor of French fries. If one were to overuse the chocolate syrup or catsup, the ice cream or French fries would lose their distinctive taste.

There are essentially three classes of modifying agents. Aromatics are ingredients such as vermouth (both sweet and dry), Dubonnet, bitters, Lillet, or Fernet Branca. Fruit juices may be any kind but without sweetener. And smoothing agents include sugar, egg, cream, etc. Keep in mind when using any of the modifying agents that they are mainly used as flavor enhancers. They add both eye and taste appeal, but use them sparingly, as their overuse may ruin a great cocktail.

Special flavoring and coloring agents include cordials

and liqueurs as well as nonalcoholic fruit-flavored syrups. An ingredient may be used as a modifier in one cocktail and a flavoring/coloring agent in another. An example would be orange juice. In an Orange Blossom, it serves as the modifier, whereas in a Bronx Cocktail, it balances flavor and color. These special flavoring agents should be measured in drops or dashes, not jiggers or ounces.

When creating new cocktails or mixing from tested and proven recipes, always keep in mind that a gin cocktail should taste like gin, a rum cocktail should taste like rum, etc. If you understand and use these basic principles at all times, you will consistently prepare great-tasting cocktails, whether for your own personal pleasure or if you decide to do it professionally.

THE WELL-STOCKED BAR

To prepare the cocktails in this book, you will need to stock up on the following items. Just as you keep staples in your kitchen in order to prepare meals, you will need staples to prepare cocktails for you and your guests.

Vodka	
Gin	London dry and either Old Tom or Plymouth
Whiskey	Bourbon, rye, Scotch, Canadian, and Irish
Rum	Light, dark (aged), and spiced
Tequila	Blanco, reposado, and anejo
Vermouth	Sweet and dry
Liqueurs	Irish cream, coffee, hazelnut, amaretto, Benedictine, orange curacao, peach, crème de cassis, and crème de cacao

Juices   orange (fresh), grapefruit, cranberry, pineapple,
              and tomato
Rose's lime juice
Grenadine/pomegranate syrup
Simple syrup
Half-and-half
Heavy cream
Lemons
Kosher salt
Ice
Sugar (granulated, powdered, and in cubes)
Vanilla extract
Nutmeg

COMMON CONVERSIONS

1 tablespoon (tbsp.)	3 teaspoons (tsp.)	½ fluid ounce (oz.)
2 tablespoons	⅛ cup	1 fluid ounce
¼ cup	4 tablespoons	2 fluid ounces
⅓ cup	5 tablespoons	2⅔ fluid ounces
½ cup	8 tablespoons	4 fluid ounces
⅔ cup	10 tbsp. plus 2 tsp.	5⅓ fluid ounces
¾ cup	12 tablespoons	6 fluid ounces
1 cup	16 tablespoons	8 fluid ounces (½ pint)
1 pint	32 tablespoons	16 fluid ounces
2 pints		1 quart (qt.)
8 pints		4 quarts
4 quarts		1 gallon (gal.)
1 liter	1.057 quarts	33.25 ounces
750 ml		25 ounces

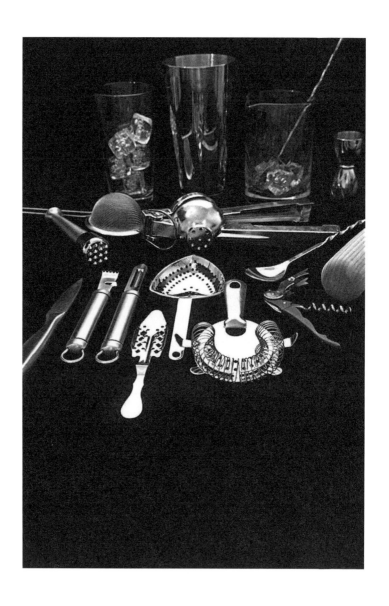

BEVERAGE EQUIPMENT

Bar spoon A long-handled spoon used for measuring ingredients and stirring cocktails. It usually measures about ⅛ oz.

Channel knife A knife with a *V*-shaped blade that is useful in creating twists. If you use it properly, you will have a zest with no pith, the bitter white substance beneath the peel.

Corkscrew A device used to uncork wine bottles.

Drink straws Large straws for sipping, generally used in tall cocktails.

Garnish tray A compartmentalized tray where cut fruit is stored for use during service. It must be emptied and sanitized after service is completed for the day. Do not use it to store unused fruit overnight.

Mexican juicer A handheld device used to squeeze the juice out of citrus fruit. It is most efficient when the citrus is placed properly in the juicer. If used properly, the result will be that the fruit will be turned inside out.

Muddler The traditional muddler looks like a miniature baseball bat. It is used to crush fruit or fresh herbs. When it is used properly, only the essential oils and juices will be extracted. Be gentle or you may release the bitter elements of what you are muddling.

Paring knife A small knife with a blade about six inches long, useful in cutting fruit garnishes.

Rail/bar mats Rubber mats lining the rail where cocktail

glasses are placed when building and mixing cocktails. They also help to collect spillage.

Rimmer   A piece of equipment consisting of three interlocking trays. The top tray has a sponge that is moistened with water, so that you can wet the rim of the glass. The other two trays may have salt, sugar, or another type of granulated dry ingredient that will add flavor to the rim of the cocktail glass.

Shakers   *Boston shaker* — A two-part piece of equipment consisting of a metal bottom and a glass top. This is used to shake cocktails to thoroughly mix ingredients and possibly create a froth. Cocktails should always be built in the glass top. This allows the guest to observe that the correct ingredients are being used. Once the ingredients are in the glass top and the bottom is securely engaged, you should be able to pick up the shaker by the mixing glass. You can then shake without leakage. The metal part may be used to roll a cocktail (see "Beverage Terms" in this chapter).

Parisian shaker — Similar to the Boston shaker but this is a two-part metal shaker with an elegant curved top. It was popular among Parisian bartenders, hence its name.

Cobbler shaker — Also referred to as a three-part shaker. This tapers at the top, ends with a built-in strainer, and includes a cap. The cap may be used as a measure.

Shot glass   A glass or metal measuring tool, also

referred to as a jigger. The standard sizes are 1 oz., 1¼ oz., 1½ oz., and 2 oz.

Shot pourer A device placed on a liquor bottle to aid in the pouring of the contents.

Sip straw A small straw added to a cocktail for the guest to stir and/or sip it.

Stir stick A plastic stick added to cocktails that is usually decorative, with the establishment's name and/or logo. The guest may use it to stir the cocktail and keep it as a souvenir.

Strainers *Hawthorn*—A device that has a spring that will fit snugly on the metal part of a Boston shaker. It is used to strain a shaken or stirred cocktail. *Julep*—Shaped like a bowl with a handle, it will fit snugly in the mixing glass of a Boston shaker. When this strainer is inserted at the proper angle, the liquid will pass through the holes in the bowl as it is poured out. The julep strainer is mainly used to strain cocktails that have large pieces of fruit or other ingredients that you do not want in the finished cocktail. *Fine mesh*—Especially helpful when you need to double strain a cocktail to remove muddled fine pieces of herbs or other finely crushed ingredients.

Vegetable peeler A tool that allows a bartender to peel citrus or other fruit. A wide twist of peel is easier to flame, if you are making a flaming drink. When using the peeler, hold the fruit over the cocktail glass to capture the essential oils that are released.

GLASSWARE

Front row: mini martini glass (2 oz.), rocks glass (12 oz.), brandy snifter (12 oz.)

Second row: Irish-coffee mug (8 oz.), whiskey glass (8 oz.)

Third row: absinthe glass with Brouille top for water drip, absinthe glass to be used with absinthe fountain and absinthe spoon

Back row: large collins glass (14 oz.), small collins glass (12 oz.), large martini glass (10 oz.)

BEVERAGE TERMS

Building

Placing all of the ingredients into either a shaker or cocktail glass, shaking or stirring to mix, and straining (over fresh ice if on the rocks, or into a chilled cocktail glass if up).

Dry shaking

Shaking cocktails with egg whites to help create froth. Place egg whites and the rest of the ingredients in a Boston shaker and shake vigorously without ice until frothy, about 30-40 seconds. Add ice to shaker and shake vigorously again to chill the cocktail. When this is done properly, you will have a cocktail with a great-looking froth on top.

Flag

Usually consisting of a slice of orange skewered with a cherry. This type of garnish is traditionally used in sour and tiki-style cocktails.

Garnish

A finishing touch added to a cocktail to give it eye appeal. It should be placed on the rim of the glass or in the cocktail on a skewer. It should not be floating on top. Also, nothing will ruin a great cocktail faster than dried-out or spoiled garnishes. Cut only the amount you will need for the day's service.

Maraschino cherry

Made from fresh sweet cherries that have been processed and packed in a high-fructose syrup along with red food coloring. They are used for looks only, as they tend to be cloyingly sweet. A better alternative is to obtain fresh sweet cherries when in season and preserve them in amaretto, vodka, brandy, or rum. They will have a superior appearance and taste great.

Muddling	A method of extracting juices from fruit or essential oils from herbs. Place the items to be muddled in the mixing glass of a Boston shaker and, using a muddler, gently crush and twist them. The key is to be firm but gentle, as you only want to extract the flavor and not the bitterness.
Rolling	A method of mixing the cocktail ingredients without diluting them. The proper technique is to build the cocktail in the appropriate glass and pour it back and forth two to three times between the glass and the shaker, just to blend the ingredients.
Shaking	Placing the ingredients in a shaker and shaking vigorously to mix them.
Stirring	Placing the ingredients in a shaker and stirring with a bar spoon. This method is generally used when only alcoholic ingredients are in the cocktail or when a very cold and undiluted cocktail is desired. You can tell when it is well chilled from the way the tin feels on your hand.
Twist	A garnish from the zest of citrus fruit.
Up	Served without ice.
Washing/ rinsing	Coating the interior of a glass with a specific ingredient, generally a flavoring agent. Add about ¼ oz. of the ingredient to your glass,

roll the glass to coat, and discard the excess. There should be just a small amount on the bottom of the glass, and the sides will be lightly coated.

Wedge   A thick slice of citrus. Lay the fruit on its side and cut in half. Cut the two halves into quarters if the fruit is large or thirds if small.

Wheels   Round slices of fruit. Starting at one end, make slices that look like wheels. Use one as a garnish for a cocktail such as a margarita or daiquiri.

CHAPTER 2

BITTERS

Bitters are the ingredients that bring zest and life to a cocktail. If used properly, they will not be noticed, but it is noticeable when they are not used. This is similar to always adding a pinch of salt to enhance the flavors when you make something sweet. You do not know it is there, but you notice when it is not.

There are a myriad of bitters on the market. Below is a list of some of the more popular ones and a brief description of each. Use sparingly and they will enhance, but use too much and they will take over the flavor of your cocktail.

ANGOSTURA

Angostura is composed of water, 47.5 percent alcohol, herbs, and spices, produced by the House of Angostura in Trinidad and Tobago. It is used to flavor cocktails and food. The bottle is easily recognizable by its oversized label, which, according to legend, was made the wrong size in the beginning but retained for its distinctiveness. Just a couple of drops are all that are needed to give that oomph.

PEYCHAUD'S

Peychaud's was created around 1830 by Antoine Amedee Peychaud, who left Saint Domingue (now Haiti) and settled in New Orleans. A gentian-based bitters, it is lighter and more floral than Angostura. Peychaud's is one of the main components of the Sazerac cocktail. It is also great in Manhattans and old fashioneds. Experiment and find your own uses.

CAMPARI

Campari is an alcoholic liqueur considered an aperitif. Comprised of fruit and herbs, it has an alcohol by volume (ABV) of 20.5-25 percent and is quite bitter. Campari may be served with orange juice, on the rocks, or with club soda and a slice of orange. It is also one of the main components of the classic negroni. Once you have acquired a taste for it, Campari can be quite refreshing and palate pleasing before a sumptuous meal.

AVERNO

A liqueur from Sicily, this bears the name of its creator, Salvatore Averno. Herbs, roots, and citrus are soaked in a base liquor before caramel is added. Averno is sweet and thick with a touch of bitterness. It is 29 percent ABV.

FERNET BRANCA

This was created in Milan, Italy by Maria Scala, in 1845, as a remedy for abdominal pain. The Fratilli Branca distillery produces Fernet Branca according to the secret family recipe of twenty-seven herbs from five continents. It is aged for a minimum of one year in oak barrels and is 39-40 percent ABV. Many say that Fernet helps relieve that pesky morning hangover after a night of overindulging. I myself don't know.

FEE BROTHERS

Fee Brothers is a fourth-generation manufacturer of

cocktail bitters, located in Rochester, New York. They have a myriad of different flavors of bitters, from lemon to peach, rhubarb, plum, black walnut, and Aztec chocolate, just to name a few. These bitters will add another layer of flavor to your cocktails or dishes.

HOMEMADE BITTERS

There are numerous other bitters on the market. Look in your favorite liquor store and speak with the proprietor to find out what is available and the flavor profile. Keep in mind when using bitters that they are concentrated and meant to be used sparingly. It is always a good idea to start with less and add more, until you reach the taste profile you are seeking.

It can be great fun to make your own bitters. It may be a little time consuming but is not rocket science. Following are three of my favorites, all of which add a little kick to cocktails. The apple and pear bitters give a great autumn flavor, and the vanilla works quite well in cream-based cocktails such as the White Russian and brandy milk punch. Just let your imagination and taste be your guide.

Most of the ingredients may be found in your favorite health-food store. If not, they are readily available from a number of online retailers.

VANILLA BITTERS

This adds great flavor to most cream cocktails, especially those prepared with vodka, rum, or bourbon. For the vodka in this bitters, don't break the bank. Use a medium-price one.

1 qt. 90-100-proof vodka

8 vanilla beans, split lengthwise
1 tbsp. roasted barley
2 tsp. gentian root
2 tsp. hulled cardamom
1 tsp. cacao nibs
½ tsp. whole black peppercorns
1 tbsp. blackstrap molasses (or more to taste)

Place all ingredients except molasses in a quart-sized Mason jar, and seal the lid. Allow the ingredients to infuse for 2 weeks, shaking the jar every day to agitate the ingredients. Once the flavors are fully extracted, strain out the solids using a fine strainer lined with a coffee filter. Stir in the molasses to taste until the molasses is completely dissolved. Store in small (2-4-oz.), dark-brown bottles that have eyedroppers built into the lids.

APPLE BITTERS

Peel from 3 Granny Smith apples, medium to large
Peel from 3 Grand Gala apples, medium to large
Zest from ½ lemon, cut in strips
2 cinnamon sticks
½ tsp. whole allspice
¼ tsp. coriander
½ tsp. cassia chips
½ tsp. cinchona bark
4 whole cloves
2 cups 90-proof+ bourbon
1 cup bottled water
2 tbsp. rich simple syrup (2 parts sugar, 1 part water)

Place apple peels, lemon zest, cinnamon, allspice, coriander, cassia, cinchona bark, and cloves in a 1-qt. glass container with a tight-fitting lid. Add the bourbon, making sure all ingredients are completely submerged (add more bourbon if necessary). Seal and store at room temperature out of direct sunlight for 2 weeks, shaking vigorously every day to mix up ingredients. After 2 weeks, strain the liquid through cheesecloth into another clean 1-qt. glass jar, squeezing to remove excess liquid from the solids. Seal the jar and set aside.

Place the solids in a small saucepan. Add the water and bring to a boil over medium to high heat. Cover, reduce heat to low, and simmer for 10 minutes. Remove from heat and cool completely.

Pour the contents of the saucepan into a clean 1-qt. glass jar, including the solids. Store at room temperature for 1 week, shaking once a day. After 1 week, strain the contents through cheesecloth to remove the solids, squeezing to extract as much of the liquid as possible.

Add this liquid to the bourbon mixture, and add the rich simple syrup. Shake to combine and let stand 3 days. Strain through cheesecloth lined with a coffee filter to remove any debris. Place in 2-4-oz., dark glass bottles and use within a year for best flavor.

PEAR BITTERS

1 vanilla bean
3 Bartlett pears, cored and finely chopped
Zest from 1 lemon, cut in thin strips
1 cinnamon stick

¼ tsp. whole allspice
¼ tsp. black peppercorns
½ tsp. cinchona bark
¼ tsp. calamus root
3-in. piece fresh ginger, peeled and coarsely
chopped
2 cups 90-100-proof good-quality vodka
1 cup bottled water
2 tbsp. rich simple syrup (2 parts sugar, 1 part water)

Split vanilla bean lengthwise and scrape out seeds. Place vanilla pods and seeds, pear, lemon zest, cinnamon, allspice, peppercorns, cinchona bark, calamus root, and ginger in a 1-qt. glass jar with a tight-fitting lid. Add the vodka, making sure that all ingredients are covered, adding more vodka if necessary. Seal and store at room temperature out of direct sunlight for 2 weeks, shaking once a day to agitate the ingredients.

After 2 weeks, strain the liquid through cheesecloth into a clean glass jar with a tight-fitting lid, squeezing to remove excess liquid. Transfer the solids to a small saucepan. Add the water and bring to a boil over medium to high heat. Reduce heat to low and simmer for 10 minutes. Remove from heat and cool completely.

Add the contents of the saucepan to another clean glass jar and store at room temperature for 1 week, shaking once a day. After 1 week, strain the liquid through cheesecloth, squeezing to remove all liquid. Add this liquid to vodka mixture. Add rich simple syrup, using more if necessary.

Allow to stand for 3 days, then strain through cheesecloth lined with a coffee filter to remove any debris. Bottle in

2-4-oz. dark glass jars. Use within a year for best flavor.

SIMPLE SYRUP

Many cocktails call for simple syrup, which is easy to prepare. For basic simple syrup, use equal parts of white sugar and water. Stir over medium heat until the sugar is dissolved and no grit is left. If you want rich simple syrup, prepare it in the same manner but use two parts sugar to one part water. Variations use Demerara or brown sugar in place of the white sugar, which will add sweetness and a touch of caramel flavor.

Honey syrup is honey thinned with an equal amount of hot water. It is a great sweetener for cocktails that include hot or iced tea.

Agave nectar, also known as agave syrup, is produced from a number of different species of the agave plant, including Weber Blue. It is sweeter than honey but less viscous. Most agave nectars come from Mexico and Africa. They are produced in light, amber, and dark varieties. The light agave nectar has a very mild, almost neutral flavor and works well in delicate-tasting cocktails. The amber has a medium-intensity, slight caramel flavor and is great in richer-tasting cocktails, especially those containing tequila, bourbon, or brandy. Dark agave nectar has a strong caramel flavor and makes a distinctive cocktail. The amber is the most popular for cocktails. There are also some flavored agave nectars on the market, and while they do have a distinct taste, I prefer the amber for preparing cocktails.

CHAPTER 3

LIQUEURS

Liqueurs or cordials are alcoholic beverages with a spirit base made from grains, fruits, or vegetables and flavored with anything from herbs and fresh or dried fruits to dairy products, honey, coffee, spices, etc. They are usually high in sugar content. Aperitif liqueurs stimulate the appetite, digestif liqueurs aid in the digestive process, and sweet liqueurs are great flavoring agents for cocktails or are consumed on the rocks. Many different flavors are available. Some are major brands, while others are generics that taste similar to the proprietary ones. In my experience, the proprietary liqueurs have a richer flavor and texture, but it is up to you to decide what works best for your personal tastes.

Below are some of the many different liqueurs on the market today.

Bailey's Irish Cream	A cream-based proprietary liqueur from Ireland with an Irish whiskey base. It is great on the rocks, neat, or added to coffee or hot chocolate.
Amaretto	Originally an Italian almond-flavored liqueur, obtaining its flavor from apricot stones. Some manufacturers use almonds.
Cointreau	A proprietary brand of triple sec made from bitter oranges from Curacao.
Grand Marnier	A proprietary blend of orange curacao and Cognac. This is a great after-dinner spirit.
Triple sec	A generic name for a bitter orange liqueur used in margaritas and other cocktails needing an orange flavor.
Frangelico	A proprietary hazelnut and herb spirit from Italy.

Tia Maria	A coffee-flavored liqueur from the Caribbean with a rum base and a hint of vanilla.
Drambuie	A scotch-based proprietary liqueur flavored with heather honey and herbs. It serves as the base for the Rusty Nail and is also quite good in hot tea.
Kahlua	A Mexican coffee-flavored spirit with a rum base. It is the base spirit in White Russians and Black Russians.
Midori	A proprietary Japanese melon liqueur.
Pimm's No. 1	A gin-based spirit from Great Britain.
Chambord	A French black-raspberry liqueur.
St. Germain	An elderflower liqueur used mainly as a flavoring agent.
Domaine de Canton	A ginger-vanilla liqueur with a Cognac base.
Crème de menthe	A mint-flavored liqueur, available in green and light (clear) versions. It makes a good digestif and is used in a variety of cocktails.
Crème de cacao	A chocolate-flavored liqueur, available in dark and light (clear) versions. It is used as a flavoring agent in a number of cocktails.
Schnapps	Available in a variety of flavors, including peach, sour apple, peppermint, and root beer. Schnapps are good as shots or as flavoring agents in any number of cocktails, such as the Fuzzy Navel or sour-apple martini.
Maraschino	A bitter, cherry-flavored liqueur made from the stems, flesh, pits, and even leaves of the marasca cherries of Dalmatia

and northeastern Italy. A great flavoring agent, this should be used sparingly so as not to overpower the cocktail.

Galliano An Italian proprietary liqueur flavored with herbs and spices.

Benedictine A secret blend of twenty-seven herbs and spices, created in sixteenth-century France by the Benedictine monks.

B&B Benedictine blended with brandy.

Chartreuse A cordial flavored with a over a hundred herbs, fruits, and spices. The green version is 110 proof and the yellow is milder, at 80 proof. Chartreuse has a very distinctive flavor that is an acquired taste. Green chartreuse is used in cocktails as a flavoring agent. Both versions make a great digestif.

Fruit brandy A sweet cordial in many flavors, such as cherry, peach, or apricot. It is good to sip after dinner with coffee or mixed with soda on ice.

Licor 43 A proprietary spirit from Spain with forty-three ingredients, including fruit juices, vanilla, aromatic herbs, and spices. The flavor is sweet, warm, and complex. Experiment with Licor 43 in place of orange curacao.

Kummel One of the oldest liqueurs in the world, with its roots tracing back to Holland in the 1500s. Kummel has a neutral-spirit base similar to vodka and is flavored with caraway and a number of secret ingredients.

CHAPTER 4

JANUARY: SPARKLING COCKTAILS

(Courtesy of Hotel Monteleone)

A traditional way to ring in the new year is with some bubbles and sparkles. The best way to do that is with Champagne or sparkling wine. The name "Champagne" applies only to a particular type of sparkling wine that is produced in the Champagne region of France. Considered to be the father of Champagne was a Franciscan monk by the name of Dom Perignon, and one of the great Champagnes bears his name to this day. Dom Perignon developed the process of bottling the wine so that the carbon dioxide, a product of fermentation, remains in the bottle. When the bottle is uncorked, the pressure is released and—voilà— we have bubbles.

Champagne is a blend of different grape varieties: pinot noir, pinot meunier, and chardonnay. There are several steps in the process of producing sparkling wine by *methode champenoise,* which we will only briefly go into, as it is a very laborious process. The first step is to prepare a base wine that is both dry and still (no bubbles). The primary goal at this stage is to create alcohol, and the process is very much like the one followed to produce table wine. The grapes are crushed, pressed, and fermented, and the carbon dioxide is released into the atmosphere. Aging may take place in either oak barrels or stainless-steel tanks. Once the aging is done, different wines may be blended to produce the *cuvee,* or final base for the Champagne.

The next step is to pour the base wine into bottles, usually the same ones that will be used to sell the Champagne. A mixture of yeast and sugar is added to create a *liqueur de tirage,* and the bottles are then capped with crowns that are similar to beer-bottle tops. The yeast begins to consume the sugar and produces a small amount of alcohol and carbon dioxide. The amount of sugar added will determine how much carbon dioxide is produced. Due to the cap, the carbon dioxide cannot escape, so it will eventually dissolve into the wine. A tremendous amount of pressure can build up in a bottle of Champagne, typically about 115 pounds per square inch, which is more than what is found in a tire on an eighteen-wheeler truck.

Once Champagne has been produced, it needs to be aged. The yeasts cells that consumed all the sugar sink to the bottom of the bottle and form a sediment called lees. Many winemakers allow their wines to age with the lees, as it tends to give the wine a creamy mouth feel. Once the aging process is finished, the Champagne is ready to drink, except for the challenge of removing the lees without losing the carbonation.

The solution is a process called "riddling" (*remuage* in French). The idea is to make the lees form a yeast plug, which can be done by simply upending the bottle and letting gravity do its work. However, this is very time consuming, and let's face it, we do not want to wait. So the winemaker assists gravity by rotating the bottles, helping the yeast cells to congregate in the necks.

Then the winemaker will begin the final stage of *methode champenoise,* called disgorgement (*degorgement* in French). The necks of the bottles are dipped into a freezing liquid, causing the wine that surrounds the yeast plugs to freeze. This prevents the yeast plugs from falling back into the wine when the bottles are turned right side up.

Once each bottle is upright, it is uncapped, and the pressure of the carbon dioxide forces the yeast plug out. Before the wine loses its carbonation, it is "dosed," which means liquid is added back into the bottle to fill it to the appropriate level for sale. Then a cork is inserted, kept in place by a wire cage. When uncorking a bottle of Champagne, always loosely hold a napkin over the cork. This will prevent it from flying across the room and possibly harming someone.

There are different sweetness levels of Champagne.

Brut Nature	No sugar is added.
Extra Brut	A minimal amount of sugar is added that is barely tasted. This is the most popular style produced.
Extra Dry or Extra Sec	Some sugar is added, making the wine "dry." This is the second most popular style produced.
Sec	Although the literal translation of *sec* is "dry," this style is semisweet.
Demi-Sec	Translated as "semi-dry," these Champagnes will be quite sweet.
Doux	A heavy dose of sugar is added, and this is considered a sweet wine.

There are three other methods of producing sparkling wines. The charmat method involves fermenting in large, pressurized, stainless-steel tanks rather than in the bottles. The finished wine is then bottled under pressure to maintain its carbonation level.

The transfer method is a variation of *methode champenoise*, where the base wine is fermented in the bottles. Instead of riddling the bottles, the wine is emptied into a pressurized vessel, which blends all of the wines. The wine is then clarified under pressure, rebottled, and dosed. Sparkling wines produced with this method will be labeled *Fermented in the Bottle* rather than *Fermented in This Bottle.* Forced carbonation is the least popular method of producing sparkling wine. Instead of creating carbonation by the natural activity of the yeast on the sugar, the base wine is placed in a pressurized tank. As the gas has nowhere to escape, it dissolves into the wine. The result is then bottled under pressure. This method usually produces low-quality sparkling wines.

No matter what it is called—Champagne, sparkling wine, cava (Spanish), Prosecco (Italian), or bubbles—there will always be a celebration when a bottle is uncorked. For a great way to begin the new year, let's check out some ways to enhance the bubbly by adding a few tasty ingredients.

Note: Each recipe in this book yields one cocktail unless otherwise noted.

CHAMPAGNE AND STRAWBERRIES

For a classic gesture that may score you points in the romance department, pair ice-cold Champagne with fresh, sweet strawberries, if available. Chocolate-covered strawberries are even better. This "recipe" is very easy.

Ice down your favorite Champagne or sparkling wine. Place your strawberries on a plate. Serve the wine in chilled Champagne flutes. Drop a strawberry into each glass, or feed them to each other for a truly romantic experience.

GRAND MIMOSA

This is a great brunch cocktail that gives you vitamin C along with your wine. It is very easy to prepare for those who want a little extra kick in their mimosa.

¼ oz. orange liqueur (such as Ferrand Dry Curacao)
1 oz. fresh orange juice
5 oz. Champagne or sparkling wine

Pour liqueur and juice into a Champagne flute. Top with sparkling wine. Sip and have a grand time.

KIR ROYALE

1 oz. crème de cassis or black-raspberry liqueur
5 oz. Champagne or sparkling wine
1 twist lemon

Pour crème de cassis or black-raspberry liqueur into a Champagne flute. Top with sparkling wine, and garnish with lemon twist.

FRENCH 75

This cocktail traces its origins to World War I France and is named after the French 75mm gun. There is some controversy over whether the first French 75 was made with cognac or gin. I think it was cognac, as it was created in France and cognac was more prevalent. Whichever way you like it, the French 75 is a great cocktail to celebrate not just the new year but every day of January.

½ oz. cognac or gin
½ oz. fresh lemon juice
¼ oz. simple syrup (more or less to taste)
5 oz. Champagne or sparkling wine
1 twist lemon

Pour cognac or gin, juice, and simple syrup into an ice-filled mixing glass and stir to chill. Strain into a Champagne flute. Top with Champagne or sparkling wine and garnish with lemon twist.

CHAMPAGNE COCKTAIL

The cognac in this recipe is optional, but it will give more depth to the cocktail.

>   1 cube sugar
>   3-4 drops Angostura bitters
>   ¼ oz. cognac
>   5 oz. Champagne or sparkling wine
>   1 twist lemon

Place sugar cube in bottom of Champagne flute. Add bitters and cognac; stir until the sugar cube is dissolved. Top with Champagne or sparkling wine. Be careful and add this slowly, so as not to overflow the glass. When the carbonation of the wine mixes with the sugar, it will create more carbonation. You may need to pause and add more once the bubbles settle down. Garnish with lemon twist.

BELLINI

The Bellini traces its roots to Italy, where for a short time the white peach is in season. If you are fortunate enough to have the elusive white peach, puree and sweeten it to taste. If it is not available, a great substitute is to combine equal parts fresh orange juice and peach liqueur (Mathilde Peche is a good one). It won't be quite as delicate as using a white peach puree but will be tasty just the same.

>   ½ oz. white peach puree
>   5 oz. Champagne or sparkling wine

Place puree in a Champagne flute and top with Champagne or sparkling wine.

DEATH IN THE AFTERNOON

This was a favorite of Ernest Hemingway. After a couple of these, you may write the next great American novel.

½ oz. absinthe
5-6 oz. Champagne or sparkling wine
1 twist lemon (optional)

Pour absinthe in a Champagne flute and top with ice-cold Champagne or sparkling wine. Garnish with lemon twist if desired.

FRENCH 007

The French 007 is not named for James Bond but rather for a cocktail competition that was held in 2007 using Champagne. A twist on the Kir Royale, it is light and refreshing—great for a brunch or as an afternoon respite. It is easy to make and easier to consume. Pear liqueur gives a more intense flavor than pear vodka.

½ oz. pear liqueur or pear vodka
½ oz. pomegranate liqueur
Ice
5 oz. Champagne or sparkling wine
1 twist lemon

Pour pear and pomegranate liqueurs into a Boston shaker with ice and shake to chill. Strain into Champagne flute and top with Champagne. Garnish with lemon twist.

PIMM'S ROYALE

1 oz. Pimm's No. 1
5 oz. Champagne or sparkling wine
1 twist lemon

Pour Pimm's into a Champagne flute and top with Champagne or sparkling wine. Garnish with lemon twist.

D'ARTAGNAN

½ oz. Armagnac
½ oz. Grand Marnier
¼ oz. fresh orange juice
5 oz. Champagne or sparkling wine

Pour Armagnac, Grand Marnier, and juice in a Champagne flute and top with Champagne or sparkling wine.

SPARKLING JULEP

This is a great way to use up sparkling wine that may be a little flat, as the sugar will help revive it.

6-8 fresh mint leaves
1 oz. simple syrup
¼ oz. fresh lemon juice
Crushed ice
4 oz. Champagne or sparkling wine
1 sprig mint

Place mint leaves and simple syrup in a rocks glass and lightly muddle the mint to release the oils. Add the lemon juice and stir. Fill glass with crushed ice and top with Champagne or sparkling wine. Garnish with mint sprig and 2 sip straws.

LEMON SUNSHINE

This is very light and refreshing.

¼ oz. Limoncello
¼ oz. vodka

5 oz. Prosecco
1 twist lemon

Pour Limoncello and vodka into a Champagne flute and top with Prosecco. Garnish with twist of lemon.

NONALCOHOLIC LIBATIONS

To prepare nonalcoholic sparkling cocktails, substitute either ginger ale, lemon-lime soda, or club soda for the sparkling wine or Champagne. Peach puree paired with lemon-lime soda creates a tasty Bellini-style cocktail. Cranberry juice blends very well with ginger ale. Let your imagination be your guide. If you use the same glassware as you would for the alcoholic version, no one will be the wiser, and your non-imbibing guests will be able to enjoy your creations yet not feel out of place.

SPARKLING CRANBERRY

1 oz. cranberry juice
5 oz. ginger ale
1 twist lemon

Pour juice into a Champagne flute and top with ginger ale. Garnish with lemon twist.

SPARKLING PEACH

1 oz. peach puree
5 oz. lemon-lime soda
1 peach wedge

Place puree in a Champagne flute and top with soda. Garnish with peach wedge.

SPARKLING SUNSHINE

1 oz. fresh orange juice
5 oz. club soda or sparkling water
1 slice orange

Pour juice into a Champagne flute and top with soda or sparkling water. Garnish with orange slice.

CHAPTER 5

FEBRUARY: RUM AND VALENTINE COCKTAILS

Hurricane

February is generally the time for Mardi Gras. The date of Mardi Gras depends on the date of Easter Sunday, which means that Mardi Gras can fall anywhere between February 5 and March 12. While Mardi Gras (Fat Tuesday) is one day only, weeks of Carnival season lead up to it, with parades and masked balls. Carnival begins on January 6, also known as Twelfth Night or Epiphany, and ends at midnight Mardi Gras Night.

Mardi Gras was first celebrated in the United States in 1703 in the tiny settlement of Fort Louis de la Mobile, which is now Mobile, Alabama. New Orleans was established in 1718 by Jean Baptist Le Moyne, Sieur de Bienville, and by the 1730s Mardi Gras was openly celebrated, although not with the parades we know and love today. In the late 1830s, processions of maskers in carriages and on horseback appeared on the streets. The first official "krewe" or Carnival organization, formed in 1856 by six young Mobile natives, was named after John Milton's hero Comus. The Krewe of Comus brought magic and mystery to New Orleans with floats and masked balls. The members of Comus remained anonymous, and even today this and many other krewes continue this tradition.

In 1872, a group of businessmen proclaimed Rex as the king of Carnival, and he remains so to this day. The official colors of Mardi Gras are purple, green, and gold, and the traditional anthem is "If Ever I Cease to Love."

Most Carnival krewes have developed as social clubs with restricted membership. That is not to say they are discriminatory but rather they have their own bylaws that members must follow. Members fund their krewes through dues and also events held throughout the year. Thanks to their efforts, they are able to put on what we here in New Orleans call the "Greatest Free Show on Earth," and if you have ever experienced Mardi Gras, you will agree with that claim.

Another Carnival tradition is the king cake, which is a type of pastry made of cinnamon dough braided into a round or oval and decorated with purple, green, and gold sugar or icing. It may be plain or include fillings of fruit, cream cheese, and/or chocolate. The king cake is believed to have begun in the 1870s to commemorate the Three Kings' visit to the Baby Jesus on Epiphany. Its shape is a symbol of unity. Today, a small plastic baby is placed inside each king cake, and the tradition is that whoever receives the piece with the baby provides the king cake for the next Carnival party. Throw your own Carnival king cake party, and whoever "gets the baby" will become the king or queen of your party.

February 2006 was a memorable Carnival in New Orleans. I was a member of the Krewe of Shangri-La, and we were among the first to parade down St. Charles Avenue that year. It was approximately six months following Hurricane Katrina, which had devastated not just the greater New Orleans area but the Gulf Coast of Louisiana and Mississippi. Riding on a float in 2006 was one of the greatest experiences of my life. If there was any proof that New Orleans was up and running, that Carnival was it. The enthusiastic spectators along the parade route showed not only us but the whole world that we were back—maybe not 100 percent, but we were well on our way and not going to let a monster storm knock us down.

Carnival is the time of year when family, friends,

neighbors, and acquaintances make a point of meeting up with each other, whether on the street or in yards, to watch parades or just have a celebration. Rum lends itself to a great many cocktails that may also be made in quantity. If you are hosting a party and make some of the cocktails that follow in quantity, you can sit back and enjoy the festivities with little or no interruption.

What is rum? It is an alcoholic distillate made from sugarcane juice, sugarcane syrup, or molasses, which are byproducts of the sugar-making process. Most believe that rum is only produced in the Caribbean. While many of the well-known brands do hail from the Caribbean, Central America produces great rums, as does the United States. The only place that does not produce rum is Antarctica.

Our Founding Fathers produced rum, obtaining molasses from the Caribbean through the slave trade. The United States' rum industry faded but is making a comeback now. Louisiana has made a great return to rum production, with Old New Orleans Rum, Bayou Rum, and Rougaroux Rum all using Louisiana sugarcane. Due to growing demand, there will be many more rum producers to come.

Sugarcane itself may be traced back to ancient India and China. One of the earliest examples of rum was a Malay product called *brum*, and Marco Polo described a very good sugar wine that he consumed in what is now Iran.

Rum was first distilled in the Caribbean in the seventeenth century by plantation slaves, making what is considered the precursor of modern-day rum. At the time, molasses had been routinely disposed of as waste, but the slaves discovered that after it sat out, it would ferment into a rough but appealing spirit.

Continuous still production results in light (or "white") to medium rums, while pot stills produce medium to heavy rums with fuller flavor. The light rums are great for mixing in cocktails, and the gold (or "dark") ones lend themselves more to sipping neat or on the rocks. The gold ones make good cocktails too but can overpower the other ingredients. There is even a "black" rum, with a sometimes smoky flavor. Spiced rums are usually aged about the same duration as black rum, with spices and caramel coloring added to provide a sweet, spicy flavor. Let your own taste be your guide, as there are no hard and fast rules for these cocktails.

MARDI GRAS PUNCH

This is a very refreshing punch to take with you to a parade or to serve at your Carnival party. If you want to be even more decadent, replace the ginger ale or lemon-lime soda with Champagne or sparkling wine.

10 oz. light rum
10 oz. gold rum
3 oz. raspberry liqueur
3 oz. fresh lemon juice
32 oz. fresh-brewed cold chamomile tea
32 oz. ginger ale or lemon-lime soda
Chamomile-tea ice cubes
Fresh raspberries
Fresh lemon wheels

Place all liquid ingredients in a large punch bowl. Chill with ice cubes and float raspberries and lemon wheels on top.

HURRICANE

This cocktail was made famous at Pat Obrien's Bar on St. Peter Street in the French Quarter of New Orleans. They have not made their recipe public, but here is a close approximation.

1½ oz. light rum
1½ oz. gold rum
2 oz. fresh orange juice
1 oz. pineapple juice
½ oz. orgeat syrup

½ oz. grenadine
Ice
1 orange flag

Build in an ice-filled Hurricane or large collins glass and roll to mix. Garnish with orange flag.

COLADATINI

CARAMELIZED-PINEAPPLE PUREE

1 medium fresh pineapple, cubed
Cane syrup to taste

Place pineapple in a heavy skillet and cook over medium-low heat until it softens and starts to caramelize. It should start to brown at this point. Remove from heat and allow to cool.

Using an immersion blender, puree to a liquid. Add syrup; do not oversweeten. Refrigerate until ready to use. Will keep up to 48 hours.

FRESH COCONUT CREAM

16 oz. heavy cream
5 oz. coconut water
⅛ cup powdered sugar
½ tbsp. vanilla extract

Beat all ingredients until just thickened and cream barely coats the back of a spoon. If you overbeat, you will not be able to float the cream on top of the cocktail. Refrigerate in sealed container no longer than 3 days.

TOASTED COCONUT

2 cups fresh grated coconut

Place coconut on a flat cookie sheet and toast in a 250-degree oven for 10-12 minutes, watching carefully and stirring frequently until lightly browned. Remove from oven and allow to cool. Store in an airtight container until ready to use.

COLADATINI

2 oz. light rum
3 oz. caramelized-pineapple puree
1 oz. coconut water
¼ oz. fresh lemon juice
Ice
2 oz. fresh coconut cream
Toasted coconut

Place rum, puree, coconut water, and lemon juice in an ice-filled Boston shaker and shake until well blended and well chilled. Strain into a chilled martini glass. Float coconut cream on top. Sprinkle with some toasted coconut.

MAI TAI

The name of this cocktail translates from the Tahitian to mean "out of this world." When made correctly, it truly is out of this world. The mai tai is reputed to have been created by Victor Jules Bergeron, of Trader Vic Restaurant, around 1934. If you want to make it in quantity, just multiply this recipe by the number of servings you want to do.

1 oz. light rum
1 oz. gold rum
½ oz. fresh lime juice
½ oz. orange curacao
½ oz. orgeat syrup
Ice
1 orange-cherry flag
1 sprig mint (optional)

Build the cocktail in an ice-filled, 8-10-oz. old fashioned glass, and garnish with flag. A sprig of fresh mint also adds an exotic touch to the garnish.

ZOMBIE

This cocktail also lends itself to be made in quantity for taking with you on the parade route.

¾ oz. light rum
¾ oz. gold rum
¾ oz. spiced rum
¾ oz. 151 overproof rum
1 oz. pineapple juice
1 oz. passionfruit syrup
1 dash Angostura bitters
Ice
1 orange-cherry flag

Place all liquids in an ice-filled hurricane glass and roll into a Boston shaker to mix and chill. Garnish with flag.

DARK AND STORMY

This variation of a Moscow Mule is made with a strong spiced rum. The amount of simple syrup to use depends on the tartness of the lime juice.

Ice
1½ oz. dark spiced rum
1 oz. fresh lime juice
¼ oz. simple syrup or to taste
4-5 oz. ginger beer
1 lime wedge

Fill a 12-oz. old fashioned glass with ice. Add rum, lime juice, and simple syrup. Stir to mix and top with ginger beer. Garnish with lime.

HEMINGWAY DAIQUIRI

According to tradition, this cocktail began its life at the El Floridita Hotel in Havana, Cuba. A diabetic, Hemingway avoided sugar, but over the years, it has been added to balance out the tartness of the fresh lime and grapefruit juices. This cocktail is also known as Papa Doble. Hemingway was affectionately known as "Papa," and he liked his cocktails strong, hence the "double." This cocktail is traditionally served well chilled and up. After a couple of these, you may just be as adventurous as Hemingway was.

2 oz. light or silver rum
1 oz. fresh lime juice

¼ oz. fresh grapefruit juice
¼ oz. maraschino liqueur
¼ oz. simple syrup
Ice
1 lime wedge or wheel

Place all liquids in an ice-filled Boston shaker and shake until well chilled and mixed. Strain into a chilled martini glass and garnish with lime.

BACARDI COCKTAIL

When making this cocktail, keep in mind that it may only be made with Bacardi rum. Bacardi has a patent on the name.

1¼ oz. Bacardi light rum
1 oz. fresh lime juice
¼ oz. grenadine
Ice
1 lime wedge

Pour all liquids into an ice-filled Boston shaker and shake to blend and chill. Strain into a chilled coupe-style or martini glass. Garnish with lime.

PLANTER'S PUNCH

Planter's punch was created in Jamaica to celebrate the opening of the Myers's Rum Distillery in 1879. Some recipes call for light rum and float the Myers's Rum (a gold rum) on top. I prefer using Myers's only, as it gives a rich flavor.

1½ oz. Myers's Rum
5½ oz. fresh orange juice
1 oz. fresh lime juice
¼ oz. grenadine
¼ oz. simple syrup
Ice
1 orange-cherry flag

Pour all liquids into an ice-filled Boston shaker and shake to blend and chill. Strain into an ice-filled collins glass and garnish with flag.

YELLOW BIRD

1 oz. light rum
½ oz. orange curacao
½ oz. Galliano
½ oz. fresh lime juice
Ice
1 lime wedge

Build in an ice-filled rocks glass, and roll to mix. Garnish with lime.

BAHAMA MAMA

1 oz. silver rum	3 oz. pineapple juice
1 oz. gold rum	¼ oz. grenadine
1 oz. black rum	Ice
1 oz. coconut rum	1 orange-cherry flag
2 oz. fresh orange juice	

Pour all liquids into an ice-filled Boston shaker and shake until well chilled and blended. Strain into a collins glass. Garnish with flag.

CLASSIC COLLINS

The classic sour style of cocktail would be the Tom Collins, along with its cousins the Jack Collins, Scotch Collins, Vodka Collins, etc. All are made the same way but using different spirits. Here is the master recipe. Adding and muddling fresh seasonal fruits makes for great variations. You are limited only by your own imagination. Have fun.

1¼ oz. spirit (such us rum, gin, vodka, scotch, or bourbon)
3 oz. fresh lemon juice
1 oz. simple syrup (or more or less depending on taste and tartness of lemons)
Ice
2 oz. sparkling water or club soda

Place spirit, lemon juice, and simple syrup in an ice-filled collins glass and roll to mix. Top with sparkling water.

VALENTINE'S DAY CHOCOLATE COCKTAILS

February is not only the traditional month of Mardi Gras—it is also the month for lovers. The following cocktails are great ones for amazing and dazzling that special someone in your life.

RASPBERRY TRUFFLETINI

This is a great after-dinner cocktail. If you really want to impress that special someone, place a red rose on the side.

1 oz. coffee liqueur	¼ oz. walnut liqueur
1 oz. black-raspberry liqueur	Ice
	2-3 fresh raspberries
1 oz. vanilla vodka	Grated chocolate
1 oz. Irish cream liqueur	Biscotti

Pour all liquids into an ice-filled Boston shaker and shake until well chilled and blended. Strain into a martini glass. Float raspberries and some grated chocolate on top. Serve with a biscotti on the side for dipping.

CHOCOLATE CHERRY

1 oz. vanilla vodka
½ oz. cherry vodka
½ oz. light crème de cacao
2-3 dashes vanilla bitters
Ice
Grated chocolate

Pour all liquids into an ice-filled Boston shaker and shake until frothy and well chilled. Strain into a chilled martini glass. Garnish with a sprinkling of chocolate.

CHOCOLATE MARTINI

For an extra-special presentation, drizzle some chocolate syrup around the inside of the martini glass before adding the cocktail.

Sweetened cocoa powder
2 oz. vodka
1½ oz. chocolate liqueur or dark crème de cacao
2 dashes vanilla bitters
2 dashes chocolate bitters
Ice
1 chocolate candy

Moisten the rim of a martini glass and dip in cocoa powder. Place liquid ingredients in an ice-filled Boston shaker and shake until well chilled and blended. Strain into cocoa-rimmed glass. Drop in a small chocolate candy for an extra treat at the end.

CHAPTER 6

MARCH: COFFEE AND "SAINT" COCKTAILS

Most of us are familiar with Irish coffee in some form or another, and in a lot of cases they are not the most memorable of cocktails. They may be overly sweet, prepared with bad coffee, and/or served lukewarm with whipped cream from an aerosol can. In honor of St. Patrick, we will learn how to create a great Irish coffee similar to the one served at the Buena Vista Cafe in San Francisco. We will also learn about some other cultures' takes on coffee cocktails.

The most important ingredient in any coffee cocktail is the coffee. Make sure it is hot, fresh, and from a dark, flavorful roast. The next most important ingredient is the whipped cream. Do not use the aerosol kind or the frozen stuff in a tub; prepare your own! It is very easy. Take cold heavy cream, and for every pint, add approximately 2 tbsp. powdered sugar. Using powdered instead of granulated sugar gives a smoother consistency without the grit. Whip with a whisk until just thickened. It should be thick enough to float on top of the hot coffee but still be able to flow easily from the container it has been prepared in. When you sip your coffee cocktail, you will be tasting a great combination of rich coffee, a spirit, and lightly sweetened cream.

Many coffee cocktails predate the Irish coffee, but the original Irish coffee has been attributed to a gentleman by the name of Joe Sheridan, who in the 1940s was employed at what was to become Shannon International Airport in Ireland. As the story goes, he first served hot coffee laced with Irish whiskey to a group of Americans who had disembarked from a Pan Am flight on a cold, damp, and miserable evening. When they asked if they were drinking

Brazilian coffee, Joe responded no, they were drinking Irish coffee, and a classic was born.

A travel writer who had consumed Irish coffee at the Shannon Airport brought the concept back with him to the U.S., where he persuaded the Buena Vista Cafe in San Francisco to begin serving it.

SWEETENED WHIPPED CREAM

Use this recipe for the coffee-cocktail garnishes in this chapter.

1 pt. heavy cream
2 tbsp. powdered sugar
2-3 drops vanilla extract or vanilla bitters

Place all ingredients in a chilled bowl and beat until the consistency of honey. The cream should be able to pour but thick enough to float on top of the hot coffee.

IRISH COFFEE (BUENA VISTA CAFE STYLE)

The classic recipe for Irish coffee has only four ingredients, but as in a great musical quartet, each component must have the quality to stand on its own. The clear mug really shows off this cocktail, as the cream first forms a floating layer, then slowly melts into the hot coffee.

Hot water
1 tsp. brown sugar
2 oz. Irish whiskey
4 oz. fresh-brewed hot dark-roast coffee
1½ oz. sweetened whipped cream

Pour hot water into a glass Irish-coffee mug to heat it. Once the mug is hot, empty out the water. Add brown sugar and Whiskey and stir to dissolve sugar. Add the hot coffee and float the cream on top.

COFFEE COCKTAILS

Prepare each of the cocktails below as you would the Irish coffee but omitting the brown sugar. It is important to heat the mug with hot water before adding the ingredients, as it will help keep your cocktail hot. Remember you are only limited by your imagination.

Coffee cocktails are simple to prepare, but to create truly great ones, use the best ingredients. Using fresh-brewed, flavorful, piping-hot coffee is of utmost importance. A rich, dark roast is imperative if it is going to be able to stand up to the flavor of the spirit in the cocktail.

SPANISH COFFEE

1 oz. Spanish brandy or your favorite
1 oz. coffee liqueur
4 oz. fresh-brewed hot dark-roast coffee
1 oz. sweetened whipped cream

MEXICAN COFFEE

1 oz. blanco (clear) tequila
½ oz. dark crème de cacao or coffee liqueur
4-5 oz. fresh-brewed hot dark-roast coffee
1 oz. sweetened whipped cream

ITALIAN COFFEE

1 oz. amaretto
1 oz. hazelnut or walnut liqueur
4 oz. fresh-brewed hot dark-roast coffee
1 oz. sweetened whipped cream

SCOTTISH COFFEE

1 oz. Drambuie
½ oz. blended scotch
4 oz. fresh-brewed hot dark-roast coffee
1 oz. sweetened whipped cream

CARIBBEAN COFFEE

1¼ oz. Jamaican rum
¼ oz. Tia Maria
4 oz. fresh-brewed hot dark-roast coffee
1 oz. sweetened whipped cream

CAFFE CORRETTO

This is not so much a cocktail as a style of enjoying your espresso and liqueur. Traditionally the espresso is served with either sambuca (a licorice liqueur) or grappa (a brandy) on the side. Follow your own preference as to which liqueur you will use to "correct" the espresso. Cognac, whiskey, or any other spirit you like and enjoy will make an equally tasty *caffe corretto*.

RINSETTO

When you are finished with your espresso, rinse your cup with your favorite Italian liqueur and sip. You will experience some of the espresso flavor with your liqueur. This makes a great afternoon pick-me-up or nightcap.

CARAJILLO–STYLE "IRISH" COFFEE

In the Spanish culture, there is a coffee cocktail called the carajillo. *According to folklore, it dates back to the Spanish occupation of Cuba, where the troops combined coffee with rum to give them courage or mettle (*coraje*). The cocktail's name morphed into* corajillo *and then* carajillo. *Another story has it originating from Frenchmen loading goods in Barcelona who, rather than asking for a glass of liquor and a coffee, asked to have it mixed.* Que ara guillo *in Catalan translates to "Now I'm leaving in a hurry" and has morphed into* carajillo. *It may be served in the Italian style, with the spirit on the side. Or you may heat the spirit with lemon, sugar, and cinnamon, and add the coffee last. This is a great pick-me-up in the afternoon or finish to a sumptuous meal.*

Hot water
Sugar-cinnamon mixture
¾ oz. light rum
½ oz. orange curacao
2 oz. coffee liqueur
3-4 oz. fresh-brewed hot dark-roast coffee
1 oz. sweetened whipped cream

Pour hot water into a glass Irish-coffee mug to heat it. Once the mug is hot, empty out the water. Dip the mug in the sugar-cinnamon mixture to coat the rim. Add the spirits and coffee and top with the cream.

CAFE BRULOT

Here in New Orleans, dining out is almost always an experience. Most people eat to live, but not only do New Orleanians live to eat—we live to drink. Cafe brulot is the perfect way to culminate any great culinary celebration. It is both tasty and dramatic in its presentation. Just use caution while preparing it, so as not to burn your yourself, your guest(s), or anything around. It still tastes great if you leave out the brandy. For a nonalcoholic version, place all ingredients except brandy and coffee in a heat-resistant vessel with 4 oz. water, heat almost to boiling, and let steep for 5 minutes. Add coffee, ladle into demitasse cups, and enjoy.

2 cinnamon sticks
8 whole cloves
1-2 tsp. sugar
1 lemon peel, chopped
¼ orange peel, chopped
3 oz. brandy
3 cups fresh-brewed hot dark-roast coffee

Place cinnamon, cloves, sugar, peels, and brandy in a heat-resistant vessel and heat on the stove. When brandy is hot but not boiling, bring vessel to the table and ignite the brandy fumes with a long match. Using a heat-resistant ladle, stir liquid around the vessel. Pour hot coffee into the flaming mixture and ladle into 6 or more demitasse cups. Your ladle should have a built-in strainer to keep any solids out of the cups.

BLARNEY STONE

After a couple of these on St. Patrick's Day, you will start speaking blarney, so consume with caution.

2 oz. Irish whiskey	1 dash Angostura bitters
¼ oz. orange curacao	Ice
¼ oz. absinthe	1 twist orange
1 dash maraschino liqueur	

Place all liquids in an ice-filled Boston shaker and shake until well chilled. Strain into a chilled martini glass. Garnish with twist.

IRISH BREAKFAST SHOT

This interesting libation is more of a ritual than a true cocktail. It consists of two shots followed by some Irish-style bacon, if available. If not, you may substitute a salty ham. When you have completed this ritual, your taste buds will be convinced you just had a pancake-and-bacon breakfast. As a cautionary measure, if doing multiple ones of these, make sure a responsible person is around.

1 oz. Irish whiskey	1 oz. fresh orange juice
1 oz. butterscotch liqueur	1 slice cooked bacon

Combine whiskey and butterscotch liqueur in 1 glass. Pour juice in another glass and have the bacon ready on the side. Shoot the whiskey mixture, follow with the shot of juice, and eat the bacon.

AMERICANO

We traditionally associate March with St Patrick's Day and the Irish. St. Joseph is another saint that we celebrate and honor here in New Orleans every March. The Italian community is especially grateful to him for providing for them in their times of need. If you have ever been in New Orleans on St. Joseph's Day, you may have seen the altars that are erected throughout the city in private homes, churches, and businesses. All the food that is displayed on the altars is prepared by volunteers and given to the needy. A visitor to an altar is traditionally given a piece of bread or cookie and a "lucky" dried fava bean. According to tradition, the bean will keep you from going hungry throughout the year.

A couple of great cocktails hail from Italy. The Americano, according to tradition, was first served in the 1860s at Gaspare Campari's bar in Milan. It was originally called a Milano-Torino, as Campari comes from Milan (Milano) and Cinzano (sweet vermouth) from Turin (Torino). The Italians noted that the influx of American tourists during Prohibition in the U.S. particularly enjoyed this cocktail, and it was dubbed the Americano.

2 oz. Campari
2 oz. sweet vermouth
Ice
1 splash club soda or sparkling water
1 orange wheel

Pour Campari and vermouth in an ice-filled collins glass. Top with soda and do a quick stir. Garnish with orange.

NEGRONI

The negroni was created at the Casoni Bar in Florence when Count Camillo Negroni asked for an Americano with a little more kick.

1½ oz. London dry gin
1½ oz. Campari
1½ oz. sweet vermouth
Ice
1 twist orange

Pour liquids in an ice-filled rocks glass and stir to mix. Garnish with orange twist.

CHAPTER 7

APRIL: BRANDY/COGNAC COCKTAILS

The word "brandy" derives from *brandewijn*, the Dutch word for burnt (distilled) wine. It begins its life as a very dry, thin, acidic wine that is considered undrinkable. Once it is fermented, it is distilled and aged in oak barrels.

All Cognacs are brandy, but not all brandies are Cognacs. What, then, are the differences? The short answer is that to be designated a Cognac, the spirit must be produced near the town of Cognac, France and use three types of local grapes. Everything else is called brandy, calvados, Armagnac, grappa, marc, etc.

Cognac is produced in the Charente region of France, which is just north of the Bordeaux region. It is made from the following three grape varieties: Ugni blanc, Colombard, and Folle blanche. The acidity of the soil and the growing conditions produce the ideal grapes for a great Cognac. The grapes come from one of six growing regions around Cognac: Grande Champagne, Petite Champagne, Borderies, Fins Bois, Bon Bois, and Bois Ordinaire.

Cognac must be twice distilled in copper pots and aged a minimum of two years in French oak from two specific areas. It matures much the same way as whiskey or wine, absorbing flavor and color from the barrels. As the Cognac ages, about 10 percent of the liquid is lost to what is called "the angels' share." Most Cognacs are aged longer than the two-year requirement.

The different classifications of Cognac are:

VS   Very Special or Superior. This indicates that the youngest Cognac in the blend has been aged in oak for a minimum of two years.

| VSOP | Very Special or Superior Old Pale. This means that the youngest Cognac in the blend has been aged in oak for a minimum of four years but usually longer. |
| XO | Extra Old. This indicates a blend that has been aged from six to more than twenty years. The minimum storage age of the youngest XO Cognac will soon be raised to ten years. |

A category called Napoleon is equal to an XO in terms of minimum age and is usually marketed as between a VSOP and XO. Hors d'age is equal to an XO, but producers use the term in marketing a particularly high-quality product.

When preparing cocktails using Cognac, the VS grade is fine, as the other cocktail ingredients may not let the nuances of the VSOP, XO, or Napoleon come through. Save these to sip neat in a snifter after dinner or any other time you may want that pick-me-up.

Some different types of brandy are:

| Armagnac | A brandy produced in a region south of Bordeaux. This is made similarly to its cousin, Cognac. Even their designations are comparable: VS, aged a minimum of two years; VSOP, aged a minimum of five years; Napoleons or Extra, aged a minimum of six years. |
| Brandy de Jerez | A brandy from Andalusia, Spain. Some of these are used in the production of sherry as well as being available by themselves. |

The traditional method of producing Brandy de Jerez has three characteristics: it is aged in European oak casks, uses the aging system of *soleras y criaderas,* and is aged exclusively within the boundaries of Jerez de la Frontera, El Puerto de Santa Maria, and Sanlucar de Barrameda, in the province of Cadiz.

Calvados

Produced in northwestern France where apples and pears are abundant but grapes are not. The brandies of this region are quite tasty and should not be overlooked.

Fruit brandies

Spirits distilled from fruits other than the grape. Some of the more common ones are peach, blackberry, apricot, plum, and cherry. Fruit brandies are usually consumed chilled, over ice, or highball style, with the addition of cola, soda water, or ginger ale. A fruit brandy labeled *fruit-flavored* has not been distilled from the fruit itself. These spirits tend to be quite sweet. Fruit brandies are more expensive than fruit-flavored ones but are worth the price.

Grappa

At one time an almost undrinkable beverage, but today some very savvy winemakers in Italy are producing high-quality grappas. It is a distillation of the leftovers from wine production, but instead of waiting up to a couple of months, the grape skins are put into stills soon after they are removed from the fermenter. The distillers are careful in cutting off the grape heads and tails, resulting in a product that is not just drinkable but delicious. Even though some of the top grappas are expensive because they are difficult and costly to produce correctly, they are worth seeking out.

Marc   A type of grappa produced in France.

Metaxa   A brandy from Greece. Metaxa was invented by Spyros Metaxas in 1888. The mature Metaxas are produced from the sundried Sultana, Savatino, and Black Corinth grape varieties blended with aged wine from the islands of Samos and Lemnos. Metaxas are aged from three to eighty years. As a bit of trivia, Metaxa was the first alcoholic beverage consumed in space.

Brandies may be produced anywhere there is wine production. Whether they are called brandy, Cognac, marc, or any of the other classifications, they are all worth checking out and tasting. Ask your local wine merchant or the staff at your favorite hangout if there are any tastings around or if they will let you sample different brandies to find the ones you like.

SIDECAR

2 oz. brandy or Cognac
½ oz. orange curacao
1½ oz. fresh lemon juice
½ oz. simple syrup or to taste
Ice
Sugar
1 lemon wheel

Place all liquids in an ice-filled Boston shaker and shake until well chilled and blended. Strain into a sugar-rimmed martini glass. Garnish with lemon.

BRANDY OLD FASHIONED

1 maraschino cherry   4-5 drops Angostura bitters
1 orange wheel   Ice
¼ oz. simple syrup   1½ oz. brandy

Place fruit, simple syrup, and bitters in a rocks glass. Muddle together to release the juices from the fruit and to incorporate the simple syrup. Fill glass with ice, add brandy, and stir to mix. Sip and enjoy.

STINGER

1 oz. brandy   1 oz. light crème de
Ice   menthe

Build in an ice-filled rocks glass, then roll to mix. No garnish—just add a stir stick or sip straw.

FRENCH CONNECTION

This is a tasty after-dinner cocktail. The amaretto gives the Cognac a sweet almond flavor. Nocello, an Italian black-walnut liqueur, or Frangelico, an Italian hazelnut liqueur, may be substituted for the amaretto.

1½ oz. Cognac
1½ oz. amaretto
Ice

Build in an-ice filled rocks glass and give a gentle stir to mix.

IRS COCKTAIL

This cocktail may not take care of your taxes, but it will make filling out those forms a lot more palatable.

2 oz. brandy or Cognac
1 oz. fresh lemon juice
½ oz. simple syrup
½ oz. pomegranate syrup or grenadine
¼ oz. absinthe
Ice
1 lemon wheel

Place all liquids in an ice-filled Boston shaker and shake until well chilled. Strain into a chilled martini glass and garnish with lemon.

BRANDY ALEXANDER

This cocktail is also quite delicious when substituting a high-quality vanilla ice cream for the half-and-half. To make that version, place the spirits, ice cream, and ice in a blender and pulse until the consistency of a milkshake. Pour into a collins glass and garnish with a dusting of nutmeg.

1½ oz. brandy	2 oz. half-and-half
1½ oz. dark crème de cacao	Ice
	Fresh-grated nutmeg

Place all liquids in an ice-filled Boston shaker and shake until well blended and frothy. Stain into a chilled martini glass and garnish with a dusting of nutmeg.

FISH HOUSE PUNCH

This cocktail dates back to 1732 and the Philadelphia fishing club called the "State in Schuylkill" or the Fish House. Peach brandy may be substituted for the peach liqueur.

1 oz. Cognac	Ice
1 oz. gold rum	2 oz. sparkling water
¾ oz. peach liqueur	1 lemon wheel
¼ oz. simple syrup	

Place all liquids except water in an ice-filled Boston shaker and shake until blended. Strain into an ice-filled collins glass and top with the water. Garnish with lemon.

THE OLYMPIAN

1½ oz. Cognac
¼ oz. orange curacao
1 oz. fresh orange juice
3-4 drops orange bitters
Ice
1 orange wheel

Build in an ice-filled rocks glass and roll to mix. Garnish with orange.

METROPOLITAN

1 oz. brandy
1 oz. sweet vermouth
½ tsp. simple syrup
3-4 dashes Angostura bitters
Ice

Place all liquids in an ice-filled Boston shaker and shake to chill and blend. Strain into a chilled martini glass.

BETWEEN THE SHEETS

1 oz. brandy or cognac
1 oz. orange curacao
1 oz. light rum
¼ oz. fresh lemon juice
Ice
1 twist lemon

Place all liquids in an ice-filled Boston shaker and shake until well chilled. Strain into a chilled martini glass. Garnish with lemon.

CORPSE REVIVER #1

This cocktail will either cure you or send you back to sleep. A recipe for Corpse Reviver #2 appears in chapter 13.

1 oz. calvados
1 oz. sweet vermouth
1 oz. brandy or Cognac

Ice
1 twist orange

Place all liquids in an ice-filled mixing glass and stir until well chilled. Strain into a chilled martini glass. Garnish with orange twist.

BRANDY DAISY

The daisy cocktail first gained popularity in the late nineteenth century, and the brandy daisy was one of the original versions. Over the years, the daisy recipe evolved to include other spirits. Generally a daisy cocktail consists of a base liquor (brandy, gin, vodka, etc.), liqueur, citrus juice, sweetener, and soda. The margarita is an example of a daisy cocktail. The brandy daisy is also good with fresh orange juice substituted for the lemon juice. Adjust the simple syrup if the oranges seem on the sweet side. The daisy cocktail is another one that lends itself to adaptations according to your imagination and taste.

1¼ oz. brandy or Cognac
½ oz. orange curacao
½ oz. fresh lemon juice
¼ oz. simple syrup
Ice
4 oz. seltzer or club soda
1 lemon wedge

Pour brandy, curacao, juice, and simple syrup into an ice-filled collins glass. Roll to mix and top with the seltzer. Garnish with lemon.

JACK ROSE

1½ oz. apple brandy
½ oz. fresh lime juice
¼ oz. grenadine
Ice
1 lime wedge

Pour all liquids into an ice-filled Boston shaker. Shake until well chilled, and strain into a chilled martini glass. Garnish with lime.

CHAPTER 8

MAY: TEQUILA COCKTAILS

Tequila Sunrise

Is tequila the nectar of the gods? According to legend, lightning struck an agave plant and produced a sweet nectar that the Aztecs named *pulque*. This was the beginning of the spirit that we now call tequila. *Pulque* was so highly regarded that human sacrifices were made to ensure its steady supply.

For many of us, our first experience with tequila was not a pleasant one. It was more than likely in our early years of college and involved doing shots of a poor-quality tequila that not only got us very inebriated but also left us with massive hangovers. Tequila has since evolved from a shot drink into a very respectable spirit that makes great cocktails or even a very palatable sipping liquor.

A spirit labeled tequila must be produced in the Mexican states of Jalisco (where the town of Tequila is located), Guanajunto, Michocan, Nayanil, or Tamaulipas and only with agave from those states. This is very similar to how France designates spirits from the Cognac and Champagne regions. Due to Mexican government regulations, consumers of tequila can now be sure they are obtaining the real thing when they buy a spirit labeled *tequila*. Look for *CRT (Consejo Regulador del Tequila)* and NOM *(Norma Oficial Mexicana)* designations on the bottle to be assured you are purchasing authentic tequila.

Tequila starts with the blue agave. Contrary to myth, the agave is not part of the cactus family but rather the lily family. The agave takes eight to twelve years to reach maturity. Growers continuously trim off the bottom leaves to allow the heart (*pina*) to grow as large as possible. This plant is referred to as the *madre* (mother), as it will produce new sprouts around the base, and eventually these sprouts will be dug up and replanted. This usually occurs when the *madre* is between three and six years old. Each *madre* can produce six to ten babies per year. The replanted babies become the next generation of agave. The timing of the harvesting of the baby plants is vital to the quality of the agave. If harvested too soon, they will be too immature to produce quality agave, and if harvested too late, they are too tired to produce healthy plants. Unlike starches and grains, which are used in the production of others spirits, agave is self-sustaining, continuing to sprout. If the *madre* is left unattended, it will produce a *quito* (stem) that may grow as high as thirty feet. This stem will bear flowers carrying fertile seeds, the *quito* will deplete the *pina* (heart) of sugar, and the plant will dry out. To prevent this, the distiller will cut the *quito* as soon as it starts to grow, which will allow the juice to accumulate.

Once the agave has reached maturity, the harvest begins. The jimadores (harvesters) using a sharp half-moon blade attached to a long handle. This blade is used to chop the plant from its roots, and the leaves are then removed with a machete, leaving about an inch on the *pina*. It is called the *pina* because of its resemblance to a pineapple after the attentions of *jimadores*. The *pina* may be anywhere from 60 to 120 pounds. The *pinas* are then taken to the distillery to be cooked. Depending on their size, they are cut in half or in quarters to make them all approximately the same size for even cooking. The ovens hold on an average fifty tons of agave, and they are packed to overflowing to create a type of pressure cooker that will steam the *pinas*. After twenty-four to forty-eight hours, they release their juices, called *aguamiel*. The juices are collected and the *pinas* are milled, either by machine or hand, to extract even more juice. The fibers are then rinsed with water to release as much of the sugar as possible.

There are two ways to prepare the agave juice for fermentation. If making 100 percent blue-agave tequila, only the juice and natural yeast will be placed in the tank. This means that labs create a yeast from the blue agave itself. If making a *mixto*, the juice is combined with additional sugar and commercial yeasts, to speed the fermentation.

The fermentation tanks may be either wooden, in the case of older tequila-production plants, or steel in more modern ones. The wooden tanks may hold anywhere from eight thousand to ten thousand liters, while the steel tanks can hold up to seventy-five thousand. Once the yeast is added to the juice, it will start to bubble, as the yeast feeds on the sugars. The tanks may be slightly heated to speed the fermentation. Once a creamy, light-brown foam develops, the brew is ready for distillation.

Tequila distillation is similar to Cognac distillation, in that copper pot stills are used. Heat is applied to the still to create steam, and as the vapor condenses, it drips down into another pot with an alcoholic content between 20 and 30 percent. The heads and tails are discarded, and the heart of the distillate is redistilled to produce a tequila that is between 40 and 46 percent alcohol, which is 80 to 92 proof. When producing mixto, the final distillate may be up to 55 percent alcohol, which will be diluted with water or a neutral spirit before bottling. This double-distilled tequila is clear in color, much like unaged brandy.

There are different classifications of tequila:

Mixto	Tequila with 51 percent agave in the blend and the remainder made up of other sugars. Mixtos are the most popular and the easiest to use for mixing cocktails.
Blanco	Also called *plato*. This is clear in appearance and unaged. *Blanco* may be 100 percent blue agave or a *mixto*. Check the label to be certain. *Blanco* tequilas are great for mixing in cocktails.
Joven y abogado	Young and unadulterated; also may be labeled *gold*. This classification is slightly aged and may be mixed with some aged tequila. The golden hue comes from either the aged tequila or caramel coloring. This is always a *mixto* and never 100 percent blue agave tequila.
Reposado	Rested, a classifications of tequila that is aged three to twelve months in tanks of French oak or redwood. This may be either a *mixto* or 100 percent blue agave.
Anejo	Old. A label with this term ensures that the tequila has been aged up to four years. These tequilas are rested in Kentucky barrels for flavor, and by law, these barrels can be no larger than 600 liters and are sealed by the Mexican government. *Anejo mixto* are aged eight months to three years, and 100 percent blue agave *anejo* tequilas are aged one to three years.
Extra Anejo	Established in March of 2006; aged a minimum of three years in oak barrels. These tequilas are generally very smooth, with a lot of flavor from the oak.

MEZCAL

Mezcal is similar to tequila in that both spirits are distilled from agave. However, they are produced from different agave varieties. Most mezcal is distilled in Oaxaca, and the hearts are cooked differently.

For mezcal, the traditional way to cook the agave is to dig a pit and fill it with hot rocks. The hearts are added and smoked for days or even weeks. This results in a very smoky, earthy spirit. Like tequila, mezcal is very complex, powerful, and clean in taste.

Mezcals have several classifications.

Silver or Joven	Freshly distilled, clean in taste, little or no aging in oak
Reposado	Ages for one to eleven months in oak casks
Anejo	Ages for twelve months or longer in oak casks

Both tequila and mezcal make great cocktails and sipping spirits. Experiment with mezcal instead of tequila in your margarita and taste the difference. The tequila one is fairly smooth with a slightly sweet, clean finish, whereas the mezcal one will have a smoky, earthy flavor. Let your taste be your guide.

In honor of Cinco de Mayo, we begin with the margarita. As with most cocktails, there are a myriad of variations. The one presented here is the one I prefer. It is well balanced between sweet and sour and still retains the flavor of the tequila as the leading taste. Let us shake the margarita as one would shake the maracas.

MARGARITA

The margarita lends itself to many variations using different fresh fruits and herbs. It is a good idea to puree the fruit first with a little water. No sweetener should be added, as there is sweetener already in the cocktail. If you find that the shaken cocktail needs sweetener, add it to taste at that point. If you want to use fresh herbs such as cilantro, mint, sage, or basil, add it to the shaker with the ice and let the ice bruise and extract the flavor as you shake. Experiment and have fun.

Salting the rim is optional. Use a kosher or coarse sea salt, and experiment with different flavors. For example, to make a lime-pineapple salt, grate the zest of 2-3 limes into about 1 lb. kosher salt and add about 1 cup finely crushed and drained fresh or canned pineapple. Make sure the pineapple is well drained to the point it is almost dry. The salt will act as a preservative and keep for about 6 months in a tightly covered container. It is also good as a condiment. Use your imagination.

1½ oz. blanco tequila
½ oz. orange curacao
1 oz. fresh lime juice
½ oz. fresh orange juice
¼ oz. agave nectar
Ice
Salt

Pour liquids in an ice-filled Boston shaker and shake until well blended and frothy. Strain into a salt-rimmed 12-oz. rocks glass. The margarita may also be served in a salt-rimmed margarita or martini glass.

TEQUILA SUNRISE

Legend has it this originated when a restaurant owner caught a couple of bartenders drinking after their shift, and they came up with the story that they were creating a new cocktail. Whether this is true or not, the tequila sunrise is a great way to start the day and get that all-important dose of vitamin C. Using crème de cassis will result in a dryer cocktail with a little more body than using pomegranate syrup, but either way is tasty.

1½ oz. blanco tequila
Ice
4 oz. fresh orange juice
½ oz. crème de cassis or pomegranate syrup/ grenadine
1 orange wheel

Pour tequila over ice in a collins glass, then add orange juice. Give a quick stir and top with crème de cassis, letting it spread tendrils of color through the cocktail, signifying a sunrise. Garnish with orange.

LA PALOMA (THE DOVE)

La Paloma is a fun, refreshing, citrusy cocktail. When the humidity is in the stratosphere and you feel you will mildew before the summer ends, La Paloma will revive you and bring you peace like a dove. If grapefruit soda is not available, use equal parts fresh grapefruit juice and club soda, with just a pinch of salt to enhance the flavors.

1¼ oz. blanco tequila
Ice
6 oz. grapefruit soda (preferably from Mexico)
1 lime wedge

Pour tequila in an ice-filled collins glass and top off with the soda. Garnish with lime.

EL DIABLO (THE DEVIL)

El Diablo is a great cocktail for experimenting with the different tequilas. Blanco will give it an earthy vegetal flavor, while anejo will add oak and some vanilla notes. Any way it is made, the result is devilish.

2-3 fresh blackberries
Ice
1¼ oz. reposado tequila
¼ oz. crème de cassis
4-5 oz. ginger beer
1 lime wedge

Muddle blackberries in the bottom of a collins glass. Fill the glass with ice. Add tequila and crème de cassis. Stir to mix, and top with ginger beer. Garnish with lime.

DAMA BLANCA

I created this cocktail for a Don Julio Tequila competition and it was a great success. It may not have taken first place but it has become a favorite for those who want a margarita with a twist. You may want to use lime-pineapple salt on the rim to give it a little extra flavor (see margarita recipe above).

1½ oz. blanco tequila (preferably Don Julio Blanco)
½ oz. elderflower liqueur
2 oz. fresh lime juice
¼ oz. agave nectar
1 fresh egg white
Ice
1 cucumber wheel

Place all liquids and egg white in a Boston shaker and shake until well blended and frothy. Add ice and shake vigorously until well chilled. Strain into a chilled martini glass and garnish with cucumber.

MEXICAN BURRO

2 slices cucumber
5-6 fresh mint leaves
½ oz. fresh lime juice
¼ oz. agave nectar or to taste
Ice
1½ oz. blanco tequila
5-6 oz. ginger beer
1 cucumber wheel

Place cucumber slices, mint, lime juice, and agave nectar in a collins glass and muddle to release the flavors. Add ice and tequila, and roll into a Boston shaker to mix. Top with ginger beer. Garnish with cucumber.

PORT ORLEANS

I created this cocktail for an event called "Cocktails and Curds" in New Orleans, where contestants were asked to craft a cocktail to pair with cheese. I passed the first round with this cocktail. The cheese it was paired with was a semisoft cow's-milk oma cheese from New Hampshire. Satsuma is a citrus from the Southern coast of Louisiana, mainly in Plaquemines Parish. It is a mandarin type of orange. It is on the small size with a green skin similar to a fresh lime. Satsuma season is early fall and fairly short. If you are lucky enough to obtain satsumas, use them in this cocktail, but if not, fresh tangerines will be a good substitute.

1½ oz. reposado tequila
½ oz. pear liqueur
2 oz. fresh satsuma or tangerine juice
2 drops black walnut bitters
2 drops Aztec chocolate bitters
Ice
1 oz. ginger beer
1 satsuma or tangerine wheel

Pour all liquids except ginger beer in an ice-filled collins glass and roll to mix. Top with ginger beer and garnish with satsuma.

OAXACAN BURRO

Too many of these, will leave you feeling as if you've been kicked by a Oaxacan burro, so enjoy this cocktail in moderation.

1¼ oz. mezcal
1 oz. fresh lime juice
½ oz. agave nectar
Ice
4-5 oz. ginger beer
1 lime wedge

Place mezcal, lime juice, and agave nectar in an ice-filled Boston shaker and shake until well blended. Strain into an ice-filled collins glass and top with ginger beer. Garnish with lime.

SANGRITA

The Sangrita is not to be confused with the Spanish wine beverage called sangria. Rather, the Sangrita closely resembles a Bloody Mary prepared with tequila. The traditional Sangrita hails from the Lake Chapala region of Jalisco, one of the five states of tequila production. There is no single recipe, but it usually combines fresh orange, lime, and pomegranate juice if available (grenadine is a good substitute; just adjust for sweetness), hot sauce, chili powder, and fresh chopped onion and is served with a shot of tequila. The chili powder is used to rim the Sangrita glasses. Dark powdered chocolate makes a great addition to the chili powder.

There are two different versions: the *completo*, a shot of tequila and a shot of Sangrita, and the *bandera* (flag), a shot of tequila, a shot of Sangrita, and a shot of fresh lime juice. This represents the Mexican flag—white, red, and green. Either version is a great way to enjoy the earthy, fresh flavor of tequila with citrus.

As with any shooter-type of cocktail, drink it responsibly and have fun. This is a fantastic way to end a great Mexican meal celebrating Cinco de Mayo. For a different flavor profile, use mezcal in place of the tequila. It will give a more earthy and rustic taste. Like many cocktails, Sangrita has many versions and ingredients. There is no right or wrong way to prepare it.

SANGRITA JALISCO STYLE

> 10 oz. fresh orange juice (the sourer the better)
> 10 oz. fresh pomegranate juice (or ¼-¾ oz. grenadine)
> 5 oz. fresh lime juice (more if the oranges are very sweet)
> 10-15 dashes your favorite hot sauce
> ⅛ cup minced onions
> Salt, pepper, and chili powder

Combine the juices, hot sauce, and onions. Rim the shot glasses with salt, pepper, and chili powder. This yields about 12 shots. For *completo* style, serve a shot of tequila and a shot of Sangrita. For bandera style, serve a shot of tequila, a shot of Sangrita, and a shot of fresh lime juice.

SANGRITA GRINGO STYLE

10 oz. tomato juice
5 oz. fresh orange juice
5-6 oz. fresh lime juice
10 tsp. grenadine (optional)
10-15 dashes your favorite hot sauce
⅛ cup minced onions
Salt and pepper to taste

Prepare as above. For best results, prepare 4-6 hours in advance, or preferably overnight, for the flavors to marinate and play together. Refrigerate until ready to use.

TEQUILADA

This is similar to a pina colada but with a lot more kick.

2 oz. gold tequila
2 tsp. coconut cream
2 tsp. agave nectar
3 oz. pineapple juice
Ice
1 pineapple wedge

Pour all liquids into an ice-filled Boston shaker and shake until well blended and frothy. Strain into a collins glass filled with crushed ice. Garnish with pineapple and a large straw for sipping.

SILK STOCKING

This light-pink cocktail is both sweet and earthy.

¾ oz. blanco tequila
½ oz. light crème de cacao
½ tsp. grenadine
½ oz. half-and-half
Ice

Pour all liquids into an ice-filled Boston shaker and shake until well blended and chilled. Strain into a rocks glass filled with crushed ice. Garnish with 2 small sip straws.

CHAPTER 9

JUNE: NEW ORLEANS COCKTAILS

Vieux Carré

New Orleans has always been a cocktail town, beginning with the creation of the Sazerac. One of the first cocktails, the Sazerac was created in New Orleans around 1850 and was originally made with a brand of Cognac called Sazerac de fils cognac. To order one, a customer would ask for the Sazerac cocktail. In June of 2008, the Louisiana Legislature designated it the official cocktail of the city of New Orleans.

In 1886, the historic Hotel Monteleone began when Antonio Monteleone purchased the "Commercial Hotel" on Royal Street in the French Quarter. His shoe-cobbler business was located across the street. The seventy-five rooms have grown to over six hundred. The Hotel Monteleone is still owned and operated by the Monteleone family. The fifth generation took the reins in 2011 with the passing of William J. Monteleone (Mr. Billy).

One of the big attractions in the Hotel Monteleone is the Carousel Bar. The carousel was installed in 1949 and has been spinning ever since. The lounge at one time was called the Swan Room, and Liberace played one of his first gigs here. Over the years, the Carousel has hosted entertainers such as Janice Medlock, Al "Carnival Time" Johnson, Louis Prima, and Lena Prima, to name a few.

Famous authors have visited the Carousel as well, such as Tennessee Williams, Eudora Welty, Winston Groom, and Truman Capote. Capote liked to tell people that he was born in the Hotel Monteleone. He was actually born at Touro Hospital, but while staying at the hotel, his mother went into labor.

The Hotel Monteleone is one of three Literary Landmark Hotels in the United States; the Algonquin and the Plaza in New York are the other two. A number of the suites are named for authors, including Truman Capote and Eudora Welty,

In April of 2010, the Carousel hosted a 101st birthday party for Welty. Unfortunately she had passed away nine years before, but we still had a great time. *The Purple Hat*, a film based on her short story by that name, was premiered at the party. The movie's setting was the hotel's lounge before the carousel was installed.

In 1939 Walter Bergeron, a bartender at the Carousel, created the Vieux Carré cocktail as a tribute to some of the different ethnic groups that resided in the French Quarter. It included Benedictine, Cognac for the French, rye whiskey for the Americans, sweet vermouth for the Italians, and bitters for the islanders of the Caribbean.

Like many historic buildings in the French Quarter, the hotel is purported to be haunted. Whether that is true or not, the only spirits I have encountered are the ones in the bottles that are released to create the great cocktails of the Carousel.

VIEUX CARRE

This may read like a strong cocktail, but it actually mellows as the ice melts. You may adjust the amounts of the ingredients to your taste. However, make it a few times as written first, to experience its flavor. Then you may experiment.

> Ice
> ¼ oz. Benedictine
> ¼ oz. Cognac
> ½ oz. rye whiskey
> ¼ oz. sweet vermouth
> 2 dashes Peychaud's bitters
> 2 dashes Angostura bitters
> 1 twist lemon

Build in an ice-filled rocks glass in the order listed, ending with the bitters. Stir 2-3 times just to mingle the ingredients. Garnish with lemon twist.

SAZERAC

One of the first cocktails is the Sazerac, created in New Orleans around 1850 when John B. Schiller opened the Sazerac Coffee House at 13 Exchange Alley. The name came from the brand of Cognac he exclusively served. In 1870 Thomas H. Handy became proprietor and renamed the business Sazerac House. At the same time, the Sazerac recipe underwent a change as well. Peychaud's bitters was still used, but the Cognac was replaced by American rye whiskey, which was more pleasing to the local palate. Absinthe was also added by Leon Lamothe, a bartender at various establishments in the French Quarter; Herbsaint is used today. But that's enough history. Let's enjoy the official cocktail of New Orleans.

Ice
¼ oz. Herbsaint
¼ oz. simple syrup (or 1 sugar cube and 1 dash Peychaud's bitters)
1½ oz. rye whiskey
2 dashes Peychaud's bitters
1 twist lemon

Fill a rocks glass with ice, add the Herbsaint, and set aside. In a mixing glass filled with ice, add the simple syrup, rye whiskey, and Peychaud's bitters. Stir until well chilled. Empty the rocks glass; there should just be a trace of Herbsaint coating the glass. Strain contents from mixing glass into Herbsaint-coated glass and garnish with lemon twist. If using a sugar cube instead of simple syrup, place the sugar cube in the bottom of a rocks glass and moisten with the Peychaud's bitters. Muddle to dissolve sugar cube, then fill glass with ice and add rye whiskey. Stir to blend, strain into Herbsaint-rinsed glass, and garnish with lemon twist.

CLASSIC SAZERAC

This is the classic Sazerac cocktail, using Cognac in place of rye whiskey and absinthe in place of Herbsaint. Be careful with how much simple syrup and absinthe you use, so those flavors don't overpower the cocktail. There should be just a hint of the absinthe taste and aroma.

Ice
¼ oz. absinthe
2 oz Cognac
¼ oz. simple syrup

3-4 drops Peychaud's bitters
1 twist lemon

Fill a rocks glass with ice, add absinthe, and set aside. Add Cognac, simple syrup, and Peychaud's bitters to an ice-filled Boston shaker, and shake until well chilled. Empty the rocks glass; there should be a slight coating of absinthe in the glass. Strain the chilled Cognac mixture into the glass. Twist lemon twist over the cocktail and drop it in.

GRASSHOPPER

The Grasshopper was created by Philbert Guichet, who won second prize in a New York cocktail competition with it. He had purchased Tujague's restaurant in New Orleans from Guillaume Tujague sometime before Guillaume died in 1912. An interesting fact is that the Grasshopper was created in 1928, during Prohibition.

1 oz. green crème de menthe
1 oz. light crème de cacao
1 oz. half-and-half
Ice

June: New Orleans Cocktails

Pour liquids into an ice-filled Boston shaker and shake until well chilled and blended. Strain into a chilled martini glass or ice-filled rocks glass.

RAMOS GIN FIZZ

Henry C. Ramos made this cocktail famous at his bar in New Orleans. The Ramos Gin Fizz is a popular cocktail for brunch but may be enjoyed anytime. It takes some time and skill to prepare properly, but with practice, you will soon master the technique and be the envy of all your friends.

The vanilla extract is optional. I have seen it in some recipes and omitted from others. I think it creates a smoother, more cohesive cocktail. Try it both ways and decide for yourself.

1½ oz. sweet gin (Plymouth or Old Tom, for example)
¼ oz. fresh lime juice
¼ oz. fresh lemon juice
½ oz. simple syrup
⅛ oz. vanilla extract (optional)
½ oz. orange flower water (available in specialty markets or liquor stores)
1 fresh egg white
Ice
2 oz. half-and-half
1 oz. club soda

Place all ingredients except ice, half-and-half, and club soda in a Boston Shaker and shake vigorously until well blended and frothy. Add ice and half-and-half, and shake again until well blended. Strain into a collins glass and top with club soda.

COCKTAIL A LA LOUISIANE

This is a variation of the Vieux Carré cocktail. I don't know which came first, but both have great depth of flavor. The famous Restaurant de la Louisiane was just around the corner from the Hotel Monteleone. It was known for its Creole style of food, and this cocktail pairs nicely with those flavors. When this cocktail was created, absinthe was illegal, so absinthe substitutes were used. It has been my experience that most of these substitutes are on the sweeter side. To approximate this taste, I would suggest using one of the sweeter (real) absinthes rather than an herbaceous one. However, if you want a dryer cocktail, use an herbaceous absinthe. Whatever you decide, always enjoy creating your own variations.

½ oz. American rye whiskey (bourbon may be substituted)
½ oz. sweet vermouth
½ oz. absinthe
3-4 dashes Peychaud's bitters
Ice
1 maraschino cherry

Pour all liquids into an ice-filled mixing glass and stir to chill. Strain into a chilled martini glass and garnish with cherry.

ROFFIGNAC

This cocktail is named after Count Louis Philippe Joseph de Roffignac, who fled to New Orleans from France during the French Revolution. He became known as Joseph Roffignac and would fight the British with "Old Hickory" at the Battle of New Orleans. He served in the state legislature and was a banker. Roffignac also served as mayor of New Orleans from 1820 to 1828. As mayor, he installed the first cobblestone street on Royal Street and also introduced street lighting. Even with all his accomplishments, he is best remembered for the cocktail bearing his name. Although not as popular as the Sazerac, it is equally potent. In researching this cocktail, I came across a couple of recipes listing both raspberry syrup and syrup, which became a little confusing. If one were to use both syrups, it would make a very sweet cocktail. Stanley Clisby Arthur's recipe in **Famous New Orleans Drinks and How to Mix 'Em,** *published by Pelican, lists an ingredient called "Red Hembarig," which was popular in cocktails in the 1930s. I discovered that this is basically a raspberry vinegar. I did some playing around with the cocktail and found that the following makes a very palatable version.*

1 ¼ oz. Cognac
1 oz. raspberry syrup
½ oz. raspberry vinegar
4-5 oz. club soda
Ice
Fresh raspberries

Build in an ice-filled collins glass, and stir to mix. Drop in a couple of fresh raspberries.

PLACE D'ARMES COCKTAIL

Place d'Armes, *also known as Jackson Square, is a park in front of St. Louis Cathedral, which features a statue of Andrew Jackson seated upon his battle horse.*

    1¼ oz. rye whiskey
    ½ oz. fresh lime juice
    ½ oz. fresh lemon juice
    ½ oz. fresh orange juice
    1 oz. pomegranate syrup or grenadine
    Ice
    1 orange wheel

Build in an ice-filled rocks glass and roll to mix. Garnish with orange.

PINK SHIMMY

This cocktail was popular at the Southern Yacht Club in New Orleans during Prohibition, possibly due to the fact that most of the gin available at the time was of poor quality. It is similar to a Pink Lady, and its pink color and sweetness did indeed appeal more to ladies than men. This is a great cocktail for someone who does not particularly care for the taste of spirits.

    1½ oz. London dry gin
    1 tbsp. grenadine
    1 fresh egg white
    1 oz. half-and-half
    Ice
    1 maraschino cherry

Place gin, grenadine, egg white, and half-and-half in a Boston shaker and dry shake until well blended and frothy. Add ice and shake until well chilled. Strain into a chilled martini glass and garnish with cherry.

NOLA BLUES

1 ¼ oz. blueberry vodka
½ oz. vanilla vodka
¼ oz. peach liqueur
½ oz. pineapple juice
Ice
2 lemon wedges
3-4 fresh blueberries on a skewer

Place liquids in an ice-filled Boston shaker. Squeeze in lemons, drop into shaker, and shake until well chilled and blended. Strain into a chilled martini glass. Garnish with blueberry skewer and relax listening to some great blues from New Orleans.

CHAPTER 10

JULY: PISCO COCKTAILS

Pisco Sour

Pisco is a grape brandy produced in Peru. The U.S. Alcohol and Tobacco Tax and Trade Bureau just recognized it as a unique spirit on May 29, 2012. Just a little review of Peruvian history will help us understand how pisco came about and also some of the political strife that led to its demise over the years.

Around 1640 the Spanish government banned the importation of Peruvian wine into Europe, which impeded the growth of the Peruvian economy. This forced the grape-growing region of Ica, south of Lima, to focus on the production of pisco. Thus Ica became a distillation center rather than a winemaking one.

In the 1800s, Peruvians brought pisco to San Diego and San Francisco as they sought their fortunes in gold mining, and it became popular with the locals. In 1887, bartender Duncan Nicol became a working partner in San Francisco's famed Brown & Perkins Saloon (formerly known as the Bank Exchange Saloon). He restored the original name and perfected the Pisco Punch, a recipe that is now lost. According to legend, Nicol took it to his grave. I include my approximation in this chapter.

In 1903, Victor Vaughan Morris, of Salt Lake City, traveled to Peru to work for Cerro de Pasco Railway Company. In 1915 he relocated to Lima and founded the Morris Bar. It soon became the hotspot for the Peruvian elite and English-speaking foreigners, including Hollywood celebrities. Here Morris developed the Pisco Sour, using pisco, lime, and sugar. It continued to evolve until Mario Bruiget, a bartender at the Morris Bar in the late 1920s, added egg white and Angostura bitters, resulting in the Pisco Sour we know and love today. The egg white gives the cocktail a great froth and the bitters a nice aromatic finish that you smell as you sip.

It is rumored that Ava Gardner danced on the bar here after consuming a few Pisco Sours. Today Peru celebrates this cocktail with a public holiday on the first Saturday of February every year. As a sign of respect, all pisco must be consumed before the Peruvian national anthem is played.

Prohibition in the United States prevented the sale of pisco, and the spirit's popularity started its demise. Then, following a 1968 coup in Peru, land was taken from its owners and given to the peasants. These peasants knew nothing about tending vines, distillation, or running a business. In 1980 Peru returned to a democracy but faced fifteen years of brutal domestic terrorism. The few pisco brands that were still producing were often adulterated by the addition of cheap cane alcohol, because the grape harvests were small. If not for all upheaval that Peru went through, pisco could have achieved the popularity of tequila. Though they have very different flavor profiles, they are both versatile white spirits.

As a result of these challenges, even the Peruvians rejected pisco. It was not until 2000 that new producers began buying parcels of land, planting the grapes for pisco, and distilling it in the traditional, artisanal way. BarSol Pisco, led by Diego Loret de Mola, is one brand that is creating a lot of thunder and interest here in the U.S. A Peruvian native, Diego is a former financial trader who switched gears to work in the U.S. liquor industry. He cofounded BarSol Pisco, which started production in 2002 at their 100-year-old distillery; they launched in the U.S. in 2004.

Like tequila and Cognac, pisco has specific rules and

regulations for its production. It may only be made from eight particular grape varieties. All of the grapes must be grown and distilled in certain states, and every brand must be registered by the Peruvian government.

PRODUCTION PROCESS OF PISCO

Only the juice of the grape may be used in the production of pisco. The juice is then fermented either at room temperature or in stainless-steel tanks wrapped with refrigerant jackets. Whichever process is used, by law, fermentation must be natural. No yeast, enzymes, or any other ingredient (not even water) may be used. Natural fermentation usually takes eight to twelve days. After distillation, the alcohol will be concentrated to a level of 38-48 percent. The types of pisco are as follows:

Alcholado   Blended from different grapes, typically a nonaromatic Quebranta base and one of the four permitted aromatic grapes, related to some degree to the sweet muscat grape.

Puro   Made 100 percent from a single varietal grape.

Mosto verde   "Fresh green juice," distilled before fermentation is complete. Though this has a high sugar content, the finished pisco is more floral than sweet. A *mosto verde* pisco is truly a treat for the taste buds, whether in a cocktail, neat, or on the rocks.

Macerado   Includes macerated fruits for flavor. By law this cannot be called pisco, since the natural characteristics of the grape have been altered.

I would like to dedicate this chapter to my dear friend Diego Loret de Mola, who introduced me to this great spirit and inspired my deep love of pisco. I also thank him for taking me on a guided tour of Peru and its pisco distilleries, giving me a better understanding of the spirit. Hopefully you will also begin to appreciate this great spirit.

PISCO SOUR

2 oz. pisco
2 oz. fresh lime juice
1 oz. simple syrup
1 fresh egg white

Ice
4-5 dashes Angostura
bitters

Place all ingredients except the ice and bitters in a Boston shaker and dry shake until light and frothy. Add ice and shake again until well chilled. Strain into a 12-oz. rocks glass and add bitters to the top. Use a small straw or toothpick to draw a decorative design in the froth.

PISCO PUNCH A LA MARVIN ALLEN

The original recipe has been lost, so this is my closest approximation. Most recipes for Pisco Punch do not include Allspice Dram, but I have found that it adds a spiciness to an otherwise plain-tasting cocktail.

2 oz. pisco
2 oz. fresh lime juice
2 oz. pineapple juice
⅛ oz. Allspice Dram liqueur
¼ oz. simple syrup
Ice
1 lime wedge

Pour all liquids into an ice-filled Boston shaker and

shake to mix. Strain into an ice-filled collins glass and garnish with lime.

CHILCANO

1¼ oz. pisco
2 oz. fresh lime juice
½ oz. simple syrup
3-4 dashes Angostura or cranberry bitters
Ice
1 lime wedge

Build in an ice-filled collins glass, roll to mix, and garnish with lime.

EL CAPITAN

In Peru, El Capitan is consumed during the summer as a chilled cocktail, but in the winter, it is served neat as a shot to warm you up. Either way, it's a great variation of the classic Manhattan.

2 oz. pisco
1 oz. sweet vermouth
2-3 dashes Angostura bitters
Ice
1 maraschino cherry

Place all liquids in an ice-filled Boston shaker and shake to blend and chill. Strain into a chilled martini glass and garnish with cherry.

PISCOPOLITAN

2 oz. pisco
1 oz. Cointreau or orange curacao
½ oz. cranberry juice
¼ oz. fresh lime juice
Ice
1 twist lemon

Pour all liquids into an ice-filled Boston shaker and shake until well chilled. Strain into a chilled martini glass. Garnish with lemon twist.

NAZCA REFRESHER

The Nazca Lines in southern Peru are large, ancient designs in the ground created by the Nazca culture. This cocktail is truly a great way to cool off after viewing this UNESCO World Heritage Site or any other time you need refreshment.

4-5 fresh mint leaves
½ oz. agave nectar
1 oz. fresh lime juice
Ice
1½ oz. pisco
¼ oz. Domaine de Canton ginger liqueur
4-5 oz. ginger beer
1 lime wedge

Muddle mint leaves with the agave nectar in a collins

glass. Add lime juice and stir to mix. Add ice, pisco, and Domaine de Canton, and roll into a Boston shaker. Give a quick shake to mix, roll back into the collins glass, and top with ginger beer. Garnish with lime.

PINK LEMONADE (NONALCOHOLIC)

I'll close the July chapter with a recipe for a refreshing nonalcoholic beverage. As you enjoy one of these, you can keep August at bay a little while longer.

2 oz. fresh lemon juice
½ oz. simple syrup (or more to taste depending on tartness of lemons)
½ oz. pomegranate syrup or grenadine
Ice
4-5 oz. sparkling water
1 lemon wedge

Place lemon juice, simple syrup, and pomegranate syrup in an ice-filled collins glass, and roll to blend. Top with sparkling water and garnish with lemon.

CHAPTER 11

AUGUST: THE ART OF MUDDLING

When the dog days of August are truly upon us, it is time for some light and refreshing libations. The focus here will be on muddling techniques. It may take a little practice to become a master muddler, but it is relatively easy to do and soon you will want to use the technique often. The basic procedure is to place the ingredients to be muddled in the bottom of a glass or mixing cup and, using the muddler, lightly push down. With a twisting motion, gently bruise and crush the ingredients to release their juices and essential oils. You want to be as gentle as possible so as not to extract the bitterness from your ingredients or make a mush.

PIMM'S CUP

Pimm's is not only a great digestif but also very refreshing in a cocktail, the perfect remedy for the dog days of August. Maybe you've seen Pimm's No. 1 in all the bars but do not know what it is or what to do with it. This gin-based liqueur hails from across the pond in Jolly Old England and was first produced in 1823 by James Pimm to aid in digestion. A farmer's son from Kent, he became the owner of an oyster bar, where he served his secret-recipe tonic. Pimm's was served in a small tankard, and the drink was named No. 1 Cup. In 1851, he started to mass produce his spirit to keep up with demand. Over the years there have been a range of Pimm's liqueurs. No. 1 is gin based, No. 2 is scotch based, No. 3 is brandy based, No. 4 is rum based, No. 5 is rye based, and No. 6 is vodka based. Pimm's No. 1 is the most popular. No. 6 is produced in small quantities, and No. 3 has been phased out. A few great variations to the Pimm's Cup cocktail include adding muddled fresh mint, strawberries, blueberries, peaches, or any other fresh fruit that you like. You may use them singly or in any combination. You are only limited by your imagination. The cucumber, however, is an essential part of the cocktail. It enhances the flavors of the Pimm's and other fruits and adds another dimension.

2-3 fresh cucumber slices	1 oz. ginger ale or lemon-lime soda
1¼ oz. Pimm's No. 1	1 lemon wedge
3 oz. lemonade	1 cucumber wheel for garnish
Ice	

Lightly muddle 2-3 cucumber slices in a 12-oz. rocks glass. Add Pimm's, lemonade, and ice. Roll into a Boston shaker, and shake until well blended and cucumber is fragrant. Roll into rocks glass and top with ginger ale or lemon-lime soda. Garnish with lemon and cucumber.

MINT JULEP

Even though most people associate the mint julep with the Kentucky Derby in May, it is a great way to cool off in August too. Here in New Orleans, it's like a snoball for adults. Sip it through a small straw and watch the condensation form on the glass. As you consume the beverage, abandon yourself to the refreshing mint and the tasty bourbon. After a couple of mint juleps, you will feel as if you are the big winner at the Derby.

The classic julep is an easy cocktail to make but an even easier one to screw up. If you follow the guidelines in this recipe, you will become a master in no time.

8-10 fresh mint leaves	Crushed ice
¼ oz. sugar or ½ oz. simple syrup	2 oz. good bourbon
	1 sprig fresh mint

Place mint leaves and sugar or simple syrup in the bottom of a julep cup if available. The traditional cup is made of silver or pewter and is about 12 oz. in volume. If a julep cup is not available, substitute a 12-oz. rocks glass. Muddle the mint leaves gently until you can smell their fragrance. This is where granulated sugar is better than simple syrup, because the sugar acts as a grinding agent. Fill the cup or glass with crushed ice. Using crushed ice is important, as it will melt as the cocktail is consumed. Finally, add the bourbon and garnish with sprig of mint.

GEORGIA JULEP

8-10 fresh mint leaves
⅛ oz. simple syrup
Ice
1½ oz. bourbon
½ oz. peach liqueur or peach brandy
3 dashes Angostura bitters
1 sprig fresh mint
1 fresh peach wedge

Place mint leaves and simple syrup in bottom of a rocks glass and gently muddle just to release the oils from the mint leaves. Fill glass with ice and add bourbon, peach liqueur or brandy, and bitters. Pour into a Boston shaker and shake to chill. Strain into a collins glass half-filled with ice. Stir to incorporate, add more ice, and stir again, adding more ice to fill the glass to the rim. Garnish with sprig of mint and peach wedge. Sip through long straws.

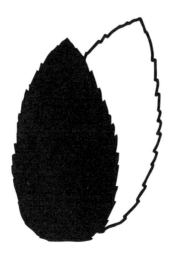

MOJITO

The mojito is a classic cocktail that traces its roots to Cuba in the early 1900s. It has become popular again, especially in hot climates. A mojito is relatively easy to prepare and there are many variations. Fresh strawberries, blackberries, raspberries, watermelon, or any of your favorite seasonal fresh fruits may be muddled for added flavor. Just use your imagination and have fun.

> 2 oz. light rum
> 4-5 fresh mint leaves (more if small)
> 3-4 lime wedges
> ¼ oz. simple syrup or to taste
> Ice
> 2 oz. club soda or sparkling water
> 1 sprig fresh mint

Place rum, mint leaves, lime, and simple syrup in a rocks glass and lightly muddle to release the juice of the limes and the flavor of the mint leaves and to mix with the simple syrup. Fill glass with ice. Top with club soda. Garnish with sprig of mint.

CAIPIRINHA

This is a classic Brazilian cocktail using cachaça, a sugarcane spirit. Look for the best ones, as they will be the smoothest. Traditionally the caipirinha is served with cubed ice, but I prefer adding crushed ice and sipping through a couple of small straws. The name translates to "little countryside drink."

3-4 fresh lime wedges
½ oz. simple syrup
Ice
2 oz. cachaça

Place limes and simple syrup in an 12-oz. rocks glass and muddle together to release the lime juice. Add ice and top with cachaça.

CAIPIRISSIMA

This is similar to a lime daiquiri, made in the style of a caipirinha.

3-4 fresh lime wedges
½ oz. simple syrup or to taste
Crushed ice
1½ oz. light rum

Place lime and simple syrup in bottom of a rocks glass and muddle to release the juice and essential oils from the skins of the limes. If the limes are particularly tart or you prefer a sweeter cocktail, add more simple syrup. Fill glass with crushed ice and top with rum. Roll into a Boston shaker and give a couple of shakes just to blend the ingredients. Roll back into rocks glass.

CAIPIROSKA

3-4 fresh lime wedges
½ oz. simple syrup or to taste
Crushed ice
1½ oz. vodka

Place lime and simple syrup in bottom of a rocks glass and muddle to release the juice and essential oils from the skins of the limes. If the limes are particularly tart or you prefer a sweeter cocktail, add more simple syrup. Fill glass with crushed ice and top with vodka. Roll into a Boston shaker and give a couple of quick shakes just to blend the ingredients. Roll back into rocks glass.

GINGER–STRAWBERRY REFRESHER

Here is a refreshing cocktail for those hot August afternoons. It is also great when you substitute either a gold rum or bourbon for the vodka.

2 thin slices fresh, peeled ginger
2 fresh strawberries, cut in quarters
3-4 fresh mint leaves
1½ oz. vodka
½ oz. strawberry liqueur
¼ oz. simple syrup
Ice
4-5 oz. ginger beer
1 whole strawberry

Muddle the ginger, cut strawberries, and mint in a mixing glass. Add vodka, strawberry liqueur, and simple syrup. Pour into a Boston shaker, and shake to mix and blend. Double strain into an ice-filled collins glass and top with ginger beer. Garnish with strawberry.

GINGER–MINT COOLER (NONALCOHOLIC)

2-3 thin slices fresh, peeled ginger
6-8 fresh mint leaves
1 tsp. agave nectar
Ice
6 oz. ginger beer
1 sprig fresh mint

Place ginger, mint leaves, and agave nectar in the bottom of a collins glass and muddle to release the flavors of the ginger and mint. Fill glass with ice and top with ginger beer. Stir to mix, and garnish with sprig of mint.

CHAPTER 12

SEPTEMBER: GIN, VODKA, AND THE ART OF THE MARTINI

The martini up or on the rocks — your choice

One of the most popular and well-known cocktails is the martini, and here we will learn about its origins and how to prepare a great one. With only two ingredients, this cocktail is exquisite in its simplicity. The garnish looks deceptively easy. Martini aficionados claim that the only true martini is one made with gin, but the vodka martini is gaining acceptance.

The true art of the martini lies in making it to your taste: dry, extremely dry, or wet and shaken, stirred, or rested. Let us first explore some of the lore of its beginnings As with most cocktails, the origins of the martini are fairly murky. The most logical precursor of the martini is the Martinez cocktail, which may have also spawned the Manhattan. The Martinez, purported to have been created in Martinez, California, consisted of Dutch gin, sweet vermouth, orange curacao liqueur, and aromatic bitters. As you can see, this is almost a combination of a martini and a Manhattan.

Over the years, using or omitting the vermouth has been left up to the individual taste of the consumer. In the beginning, the martini was made up of equal parts gin and dry vermouth. By about 1915, the ratio was two parts gin to one part dry vermouth. Today the ratios are anywhere from six to one or fifteen to one or even just holding a sealed bottle of dry vermouth in the sunlight so it reflects into the gin, or reverently passing the bottle over the gin. Whatever your choice, always use the best possible ingredients and experiment with different gins, as they all have distinct flavor profiles. Just remember that if you like it, it is right for you.

GIN

Gin can be traced back to a spirit called genever, whose

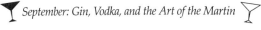

invention is often attributed to Dr. Franciscus Sylvius in the mid-seventeenth century. It was created as a juniper-berry digestif, as juniper was thought to soothe the stomach. English soldiers found that it calmed their nerves before battle and nicknamed it "Dutch courage" after watching Dutch soldiers drink shots of it and go off to war.

The early gins were much different from what we know as gin today. They involved steeping juniper berries and botanicals in a neutral spirit with sugar, oils, and flavors added to mask the harsh flaws of the base spirit.

In 1689, when William III of Orange ascended the throne of England, he declared gin the official drink of the palace. At war with France at the time, he wanted to discourage the importation of Cognac and French wines. William also relaxed restrictions on alcohol licensing, making it quite easy for anyone to distill and sell their spirits to the public. During the gin craze, there were an estimated nine thousand official gin shops in London and about one hundred thousand people who were drunk morning, noon, and night. It is reported that women pushed carts through the city streets, selling their gin.

During this period, it was safer to drink the gin than the water. It was also very cheap to make, as there was an excess of grain crops that were distilled to create the neutral spirit for gin. When those crops became harder to come by, the gin craze started to wane. But as bad as the gin craze was, with public drunkenness, child abuse, miscarriages, venereal diseases, and other problems, the spirit never suffered the bad rap that absinthe would.

The types of gin available today are as follows.

Genever	The original Dutch juniper-based spirit, the forerunner of modern gin. It tastes quite different from what we think of as gin, in that it retains a lot of the flavors of the grains that make up its neutral spirit, i.e., rye, barley, and/or corn.
London dry	Originally only produced in London. It has a high distillation proof and is unsweetened or "dry." London dry gin may be produced anywhere now, as it is a style not a brand.
Old Tom	A sweet or cordial type of gin popular in the eighteenth and nineteenth centuries. At the time, most gins were rather pungent due to the limited purification process. These strong flavors were then masked with the addition of sweet botanicals such as licorice or, later, sugar. Old Tom gin is making a comeback today, especially in some classic cocktails.
Plymouth	Only distilled in Plymouth, England, using the water from Dartmoor. This classification is determined by the European Union. Plymouth gin is distilled at the Black Friars Distillery of Coates & Co.
Xoriguer	A Spanish gin with its own European Union appellation. This gin may only be distilled on the island of Menorca.

There are two basic ways of introducing botanicals to the neutral grain spirit. The steep and boil method is similar to using a giant teabag. This is the most traditional process. Juniper berries and other botanicals are steeped in the spirits,

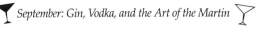

which have been diluted with water to about 50 percent ABV. The length of steeping depends on the distiller. It may be as long as forty-eight hours. When the mixture is deemed ready, it is heated and distilled in a pot still, producing a spirit filled with the flavors and aromas of the botanicals. Water may be added to bring the gin to bottling strength.

With the vapor-infused method, the juniper berries and other botanicals do not come into direct contact with the neutral spirit. They are placed in a large basket inside a modified still. As the spirit is heated in the distillation process, its steam comes into contact with the botanicals, picking up the flavors and returning them to the still as a liquid.

Every gin producer uses its own combination of botanicals in its product. It may be as few as four or as many as twenty or more. Some of the most common botanicals used are as follows.

Juniper berries	Have a pinelike flavor with a hint of sweetness. This must be the gin's predominant taste.
Coriander seeds	From a parsley-type plant and one of the oldest known spices. These have long been considered to aid the respiratory system.
Angelica seeds and roots	From a medieval herb native to Europe, related to parsley and dill. Angelica gives a bright and refreshing taste.
Lemon peel	Used to provide that citrus astringency and a clean, dry nose and taste
Orange peel	Both bitter and sweet oranges are used.
Orris root	From the Florentine iris, used as an aromatic fixative

Cassia	Also known as Chinese cinnamon, derived from certain shrubs or trees
Cinnamon	Adds a sweet heat and flavor
Cardamom seeds	Taken from plants that are members of the ginger family. Cardamom is one of the most expensive spices.
Cubeb	Berries from a shrub that is a member of the pepper family. Originally from eastern India, it is usually grown in Indonesia today, and it has been used in the treatment of urinary and bronchial problems.
Grains of paradise	Intense peppery berries from a West African plant that is a member of the ginger family. They are used to intensify the flavors of other botanicals in the gin.
Ginger	Comes from the root structure of the ginger plant. It is a common flavoring in cooking and is considered a general tonic, particularly for stomach ailments.
Nutmeg	Derived from the seed of the nutmeg tree. The seed provides two different spices, nutmeg and mace. Mace comes from the outer layer, while the interior is the nutmeg. This is the only tree that provides us with two different spices.
Cumin	A spice from the parsley family used mainly in cooking, especially in Middle Eastern countries. Cumin is also a vital ingredient in American Southwest dishes such as chili.
Rosemary	A member of the mint family, its leaves have an evergreen aroma.

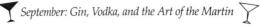

Not every brand of gin uses all of the above botanicals. The only constant is that the juniper must be the predominant flavor in the final product.

Very few of today's gins are aged. Unlike whiskey and brandy, gin does not require aging to soften is flavor. If left in the barrels longer than six months, the gin will pick up too much of the harsh wood taste. A gin should be aged no longer than two to three months in well-seasoned casks. This will give it a subtle wood flavor and soft golden color. A properly aged gin can be exquisite.

VODKA

Is vodka originally Russian or Polish? It is not clear, as both countries claim they were the first to produce it. In the eighth century the Polish discovered that wine left over the winter produced a strong alcohol. Allowed to freeze, the liquid was then used for medicinal purposes.

It was not until the fifteenth century that *gorsalka* or burnt wine was produced, as a result of the knowledge of distillation. The Polish claim that vodka was first produced around 1400 and was then moved to Russia. The word comes to us from the Slavic *voda* or water. This evolved into *vodka*, meaning "dear little water." Where vodka originated is not crucial. Just enjoy it and let the history buffs argue about who introduced it.

What is vodka? The Bureau of Alcohol, Tobacco and Firearms defines it as "a colorless, odorless, tasteless spirit of which the only ingredients are ethyl alcohol and water." There are other ingredients but only in minute amounts. Unlike scotch, Cognac, tequila, or bourbon, which may only be produced in specific countries, vodka may be distilled anywhere. It may be the most recognized spirit in the world. Vodka may be produced by any distillation process that results in purified alcohol and from any raw material that will ferment. Most vodkas of today are produced from grains.

With most other spirits you want to retain as many of the natural flavorings as possible, but that is not the case with vodka. When producing vodka you want to remove as many of the flavoring elements as possible through numerous distillations, to obtain the clean, clear, and fresh taste it is known for. Once the distillation process is complete, the vodka is filtered through anything from charcoal to diamond dust to remove the unwanted flavors.

Due to its purity, vodka will mix with anything and is the basis of many of our favorite cocktails. Unlike other spirits that have distinct flavors, when vodka is mixed with other ingredients, they become the star of the cocktail. Take the margarita, for example. In a traditional version, you will taste the earthiness of the tequila, with the rest of the ingredients staying in the background. But if you keep the same ingredients and just substitute vodka for the tequila, you will have a cocktail that tastes vastly different, with the mixing ingredients as the dominant flavors. This is not to say that vodka will not make great cocktails. But when you use vodka, the mixing and flavoring agents are very important, because they become the stars of the cocktail.

When searching for vodkas, don't rely so much on price as on your own taste buds. When you sample vodkas, look for ones that have a clean, fresh, nonalcoholic taste.

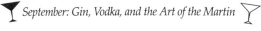
THE ULTIMATE CLASSIC GIN MARTINI

4 oz. London dry gin
¼-1 oz. dry vermouth
Ice

Place both liquids in an ice-filled mixing cup and do one of three things to chill the ingredients: stir for an icy-cold, cloudless cocktail; shake vigorously for a bruised, somewhat cloudy martini; or, if you have the time and patience, let sit and rest for 1-2 minutes. Strain into a chilled martini glass. There is no hard-and-fast rule for the chilling method—it's all up to individual taste. Many people keep their gin in the freezer and their vermouth in the refrigerator so that their martini never has an affair with ice.

The next most important part of the martini is the garnish, and there are three basic ones: 3 green olives on a skewer, generally stuffed with pimento or blue cheese, which is rapidly gaining in popularity; 3 small cocktail onions on a skewer, which will turn the martini into a Gibson; or a lemon twist to add a little citrus. Whichever you choose is up to you, so select one or all three and enjoy. Always make sure your garnishes are well chilled so that you do not warm that well-chilled martini.

DIRTY MARTINI

The olive brine is the juice from a jar of olives. If you are using vodka in this cocktail, the traditional garnish is a lemon twist to add some flavor and brightness. As we have learned earlier, vodka is essentially a tasteless spirit.

4 oz. gin or vodka	Ice
¼ oz. dry vermouth	3 olives
1 oz. olive brine	

Pour all liquids into an ice-filled mixing glass and stir until well chilled. Strain into a chilled martini glass. Garnish with olives on a skewer.

MARTINEZ

The origins of the Martinez are hazy to say the least. Some people claim it was named for a guy by the name of Martinez after he combined gin and vermouth. Others say Jerry Thomas created it for a gentleman who was traveling to Martinez, California. No one knows for sure, but we do know that it inspired the martini. You will notice that the ratio of vermouth to gin is reversed from the classic martini.

1 oz. Plymouth gin
2 oz. sweet vermouth
1 dash Angostura bitters
2 dashes maraschino liqueur
Ice
1 twist lemon

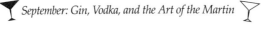

Pour all liquids into an ice-filled Boston shaker and shake to chill. Strain into a chilled martini glass. Garnish with lemon.

BRONX COCKTAIL

1 oz. London dry gin
1 oz. sweet vermouth
1 oz. dry vermouth
2 oz. fresh orange juice
Ice

Pour all liquids into an ice-filled Boston shaker and shake until well chilled. Strain into a chilled martini glass.

VESPER

One of the cocktails that helped popularize the vodka martini is the Vesper. In Casino Royale, *James Bond preferred his Vesper shaken, not stirred, and served icy cold, up, with a lemon twist for garnish.*

3 oz. London dry gin
1 oz. vodka
1 oz. Lillet Blanc
Ice
1 twist lemon

Pour all liquids into an ice-filled Boston shaker and shake vigorously until well chilled and frost starts to appear on the metal part of the shaker. Strain into a chilled martini glass and garnish with lemon.

SMOKY MARTINI

This cocktail is definitely for the adventurous and not the faint of heart. The whiskey gives a smoky, peaty essence to the cocktail. It is best to use a sweeter, less-smoky scotch from the Scottish lowlands with the vodka, such as from the Islay region. With the Dutch genever, I prefer to omit the vermouth. Whichever base spirit you use, the Smoky Martini is a treat for the taste buds. Experiment with your favorite scotch and your favorite gin or vodka, then sit back and enjoy the smoky silkiness of this cocktail.

2 oz. London dry gin, vodka, or Dutch genever
½ oz. your favorite scotch
¼ oz. dry vermouth (or less depending on your taste)
Ice
1 twist lemon

Pour all liquids into an ice-filled mixing glass and stir until well chilled. Strain into a chilled martini glass and garnish with lemon.

SINGAPORE SLING

This classic cocktail from the Raffles Hotel in Singapore dates back to 1915. There have been many versions since its inception, but this is one that I particularly enjoy. It is not complicated to make.

2 oz. London dry gin
½ oz. cherry brandy
½ oz. Cointreau

1 oz. Benedictine
1 oz. grenadine
3 oz. pineapple juice
3 oz. fresh lemon juice
1 dash Angostura bitters
Ice
1 maraschino cherry-pineapple wedge flag

Place all liquids in an ice-filled Boston shaker and shake until well blended. Strain into a chilled hurricane glass. Serve up without ice or over ice. Garnish with flag.

PINK LADY

The Pink Lady traces its origins to the 1930s and was a favorite of the ladies of high society. It is a delicately pink hued cocktail that utilizes a fresh egg white to give it lightness. If available, pomegranate syrup is best. And yes, real men will drink pink cocktails, especially if they have a great flavor profile like the Pink Lady.

2 oz. London dry gin
½ oz. fresh lemon juice
¼ oz. pomegranate syrup or grenadine
1 fresh egg white
Ice
1 maraschino cherry

Place gin, lemon juice, syrup, and egg white in a Boston shaker and dry shake until mixture is light and fluffy. Add ice and shake again until well chilled. Strain into a chilled martini glass, and garnish with cherry.

PINK GIN

Pink Gin is a British favorite. It was originally consumed for medicinal purposes, as Angostura bitters are a natural stomach settler. With only two ingredients, it is of utmost importance that you select a gin of the highest quality that fits your taste preference.

3-4 drops Angostura bitters
3 oz. London dry gin
¼ oz. sparkling water (optional)
Ice
1 twist lemon

Place the Angostura bitters in a well-chilled martini glass and roll to coat the glass. Pour the gin and sparkling water, if using, into an ice-filled mixing glass and stir until well chilled. Strain into the bitters-coated glass. You should have a slightly pink cocktail. Garnish with lemon.

WHITE LADY

The White Lady is also known as the Delilah or the Chelsea Sidecar. It has been forgotten but hopefully will be remembered again for its fresh, citrusy taste.

2 oz. London dry gin   Ice
1 oz. Cointreau   1 lemon twist or wedge
1 oz. fresh lemon juice

Pour all liquids into an ice-filled Boston shaker and shake until well chilled. Strain into a chilled martini glass and garnish with lemon.

TWENTIETH CENTURY

This cocktail is reputed to have been created in 1939 by a C. A. Tuck and named after an express train that ran between New York City and Chicago. It is an intriguing blend of chocolate and citrus that hits your tastes buds all over—truly a unique sensation.

1½ oz. London dry gin
¾ oz. dry vermouth
½ oz. light crème de cacao
½ oz. fresh lemon juice
Ice
1 twist lemon

Pour all liquids into an ice-filled Boston shaker and shake until well chilled. Strain into a chilled martini glass and garnish with lemon.

SILVER BULLET

This may also be made using vodka instead of gin. Try it both ways and decide which one you prefer.

1½ oz. gin   Ice
½ oz. Kummel liqueur   1 lemon wedge
½ oz. fresh lemon juice

Pour all liquids into an ice-filled Boston shaker and shake until well chilled. Strain into a chilled martini glass, and garnish with lemon.

SATAN'S WHISKERS

This is a variation on the Bronx Cocktail, with a more pronounced orange tang.

> 1 oz. London dry gin
> 1 oz. dry vermouth
> 1 oz. sweet vermouth
> ½ oz. Grand Marnier
> 1 oz. fresh orange juice
> 1-2 dashes orange bitters
> Ice
> 1 twist orange

Pour all liquids into an ice-filled Boston shaker and shake until well chilled and blended. Strain into a chilled martini glass. Garnish with orange.

ALEXANDER WITH GIN

> ¾ oz. gin   ¾ oz. half-and-half
> ¾ oz. light crème de   Ice
>   cacao

Pour all liquids into an ice-filled Boston shaker and shake until well chilled. Strain into a chilled martini glass.

MAIDEN'S PRAYER

The lemon balances the sweetness of the orange juice and orange curacao in this pleasant, citrusy cocktail.

1 oz. gin
1 oz. orange curacao
½ oz. fresh orange juice
½ oz. fresh lemon juice
Ice
1 twist orange

Pour all liquids into an ice-filled Boston shaker and shake until well chilled. Strain into a chilled martini glass. Garnish with orange.

SAGE APPLE

This refreshing cocktail is delightfully subtle.

3-4 fresh sage leaves
Ice
1½ oz. vodka
1½ oz. dry vermouth
¾ oz. apple juice
1 fresh sage leaf for garnish

Lightly bruise the sage leaves with your muddler in the bottom of a Boston shaker. Add ice and liquids and shake until well chilled and blended. Double strain into a chilled martini glass. Garnish with sage leaf floating on top.

FLEUR DE LIS

This was created by Parker Davis, a bartender at the Carousel Bar in the historic Hotel Monteleone. The Fleur de Lis is a light and refreshing cocktail to be enjoyed anytime, but especially in September, when summer lingers on.

> 2 slices cucumber
> Ice
> 1¼ oz. gin
> ¼ oz. elderflower liqueur
> ½ oz. fresh lime juice
> ¼ oz. simple syrup
> 3-4 oz. ginger ale
> 1 lime wedge

Using a muddler, break the cucumber up into small pieces in the bottom of a Boston shaker. Add ice and the liquids, except the ginger ale. Shake until well blended and chilled. Pour into a rocks glass. Do not strain the cocktail, as you want the cucumber in the glass. Top with ginger ale. Garnish with lime.

SCREWDRIVER

This is a great way to get your vitamin C. The name is rumored to have come from some oilfield workers who stirred this cocktail with a screwdriver. I'm not sure whether that is true or not, but it does make a good story.

> 1½ oz. vodka
> 5 oz. fresh orange juice

Ice
1 orange wheel

Build in an ice-filled rocks glass, stir to mix, and garnish with orange.

HARVEY WALLBANGER

This was very popular in the 1970s. It was reportedly named after a California surfer called Harvey who had a particularly bad day. After a few of these, he began running into walls. So take care when indulging in this cocktail!

Ice   4-5 oz. fresh orange juice
1¼ oz. vodka   ¼ oz. Galliano

Fill an 8-oz. rocks glass with ice and add vodka and orange juice. Stir to mix, and float Galliano on top.

GREYHOUND OR SALTY DOG

This cocktail is also good substituting gin for the vodka.

1¼ oz. vodka
5 oz. fresh grapefruit juice
Ice
Salt (optional)

Pour vodka and juice over ice in a rocks glass. For a Salty Dog, first rim the glass with salt, then build as above.

SEABREEZE

1¼ oz. vodka
2 oz. fresh grapefruit juice
3 oz. cranberry juice
Ice
1 lime wedge

Build in an ice-filled rocks glass, starting with the vodka and grapefruit juice and topping with the cranberry juice. Don't stir, as you want to let the cranberry juice filter through the cocktail for a colorful effect. Garnish with lime.

BAY BREEZE

Sip this and you will feel as though you are on the beach of some Caribbean island.

1¼ oz. vodka
3 oz. pineapple juice
2 oz. cranberry juice
Ice
1 fresh pineapple wedge

Build in an ice-filled rocks glass, beginning with the vodka and pineapple juice and topping with the cranberry juice. Don't stir, as you want to let the cranberry juice filter through the cocktail for a colorful effect. Garnish with pineapple.

HANKY-PANKY

The Hanky-Panky comes to us from the Savoy Hotel in London. The Savoy Bar hails back to 1893 and has been serving great cocktails ever since. This one was created by Ada Coleman for Noel Coward's mentor, Sir Charles Hawtrey. After taking his first sip, he exclaimed, "By Jove! That is the real hank-panky." The orange twist is vital to bringing the flavors together and making this a cocktail worth tasting.

1½ oz. gin
1½ oz. sweet vermouth
⅛ oz. Fernet Branca bitters
Ice
1 small twist orange

Pour all liquids into an ice-filled mixing glass and stir until well chilled. Strain into a chilled martini glass and garnish with orange.

CLOVER CLUB

3 oz. London dry gin
½ tsp. simple syrup
1 oz. fresh lime juice
1 fresh egg white
Ice

Place all liquids in a Boston shaker and shake until frothy. Add ice and shake again until well chilled. Strain into a chilled rocks glass.

LONDON TRAM

2 oz. London dry gin	1 fresh egg white
1 oz. orange curacao	Ice
1 oz. fresh lemon juice	Sugar
½ oz. agave nectar	1 lemon wheel

Pour all liquids into a Boston shaker and shake until frothy. Add ice and shake again until well chilled. Strain into a chilled, sugar-rimmed martini glass. Garnish with lemon.

GIN RICKEY

Said to be created at Shoomaker's bar in Washington, D.C. in the 1880s, this cocktail was named after Col. Joe Rickey. It may be prepared with gin, vodka, rum, or tequila, depending on your preference. The Rickey is similar to a Collins but uses lime juice in place of lemon juice.

> 1 oz. gin
> ½ oz. fresh lime juice
> ¼ oz. simple syrup (or to taste depending on tartness of limes)
> Ice
> 2 oz. club soda
> 1 wide lime peel

Place gin, lime juice, and simple syrup in an ice-filled Boston shaker and shake to chill and blend. Strain into an ice-filled rocks glass and top with club soda. Garnish with swath of lime peel.

GIN BUCK

A Buck is basically a Rickey prepared with ginger ale. It can be made with any liquor you like. Fresh lemon may be substituted for the lime if you prefer.

Ice
½ fresh lime

1½ oz. gin
4 oz. ginger ale

Fill a rocks glass with ice. Squeeze in lime and drop shell into glass. Add gin and stir. Top with ginger ale.

GIMLET

2 oz. London dry gin
or vodka

1 oz. Rose's lime juice
Ice

Build in an ice-filled rocks glass and stir to mix.

LEMON DROP MARTINI

2 oz. citrus vodka
1 oz. limoncello
1 oz. fresh lemon juice
¼ oz. simple syrup or more to taste
Ice
Sugar
1 lemon wheel

Pour all liquids into an ice-filled Boston shaker and shake until well chilled. Strain into a sugar-rimmed, chilled martini glass. Garnish with lemon.

COSMOPOLITAN

2 oz. citrus vodka
1 oz. orange curacao
½ oz. cranberry juice
Ice
1 lime wedge

Pour all liquids into an ice-filled Boston shaker and shake until well chilled. Strain into a chilled martini glass. Garnish with lime.

WOO WOO

This cocktail returns us to the 1970s, when disco was king and cocktails were sweet. Put on your platform shoes and "woo woo" as if you're on a lighted dance floor.

1¼ oz. vodka
¾ oz. peach liqueur
4 oz. cranberry juice
Ice
1 lime wedge

Pour all liquids into an ice-filled Boston shaker and shake until well blended and chilled. Strain into an ice-filled collins glass and garnish with lime.

MOSCOW MULE

This cocktail helped introduce vodka into mainstream

America in the 1940s. It was created by John Martin and Jack Morgan, who owned the Cock 'n' Bull restaurant in Hollywood, California. It was originally made in copper mugs. If you have those, use them to wow your guests. If not, rocks glasses work just as well. If you want a hot mule, gently heat the ginger beer, build the cocktail in an Irish-coffee mug with no ice, and add a couple of dashes of vanilla bitters.

1¼ oz. vodka
4 oz. ginger beer
¼ oz. fresh lime juice
Ice
1 lime wedge

Pour all liquids into an ice-filled rocks glass. Garnish with lime.

FRENCH MARTINI

2 oz. vodka
1 oz. raspberry liqueur
1 oz. pineapple juice
Ice
1 oz. sparkling wine
3-4 fresh raspberries

Place vodka, raspberry liqueur, and pineapple juice in an ice-filled Boston shaker and shake until well chilled. Strain into a chilled martini glass. Top with the sparkling wine and garnish with raspberries on a skewer.

BREAKFAST MARTINI

The following martini is great for a brunch and simple to prepare. Using the best orange marmalade will ensure that your cocktail tastes as delicious as it sounds. If available, grapefruit marmalade makes a great variation.

2 oz. London dry gin
1 tsp. orange marmalade
½ oz. orange curacao
½ oz. fresh lemon juice
Ice

Place all ingredients in a Boston shaker, and shake until well blended and icy cold. Double strain (strain from the shaker through a second strainer) into a chilled martini glass.

BRASS MONKEY

This is an amped-up Harvey Wallbanger.

1½ oz. vodka
½ oz. light rum
4 oz. fresh orange juice
Ice
½ oz. Galliano

Place vodka, rum, and orange juice in a mixing glass filled with ice. Stir until well chilled. Strain into an ice-filled rocks glass and float Galliano on top.

GOLDFINGER

1½ oz. vodka   Ice
¾ oz. Galliano   1 pineapple wedge
2 oz. pineapple juice

Build in an ice-filled rocks glass, and stir to mix. Garnish with pineapple.

KNOCKOUT COCKTAIL

This is an interesting combination of flavors.

¾ oz. gin   ⅛ oz. light crème de menthe
¾ oz. dry vermouth   Ice
¾ oz. absinthe   1 maraschino cherry

Pour all liquids into an ice-filled mixing glass and stir until well chilled. Strain into a chilled martini glass. Garnish with cherry.

MELON BALL

1 oz. vodka
1 oz. Midori melon liqueur
3 oz. fresh orange juice
Ice
1 orange wheel

Pour all liquids into an ice-filled rocks glass, and roll to mix. Garnish with orange.

BLOODY MARY

A Bloody Mary is perfect in the morning after a night of imbibing or in the afternoon as a pick-me-up. As with most cocktails, its origins are murky. Some claim the Blood Mary first appeared at the New York Bar in Paris, a favorite haunt of Ernest Hemingway and other Americans. Others assert that comedian George Jessel created it at the 21 Club in New York, where he was a regular. Either way, it has become a classic cocktail.

There is not a definitive recipe for the Bloody Mary, yet it always has a base of tomato juice, black pepper, cayenne pepper, and Worcestershire sauce. Then let your imagination take over. Some use vegetable purees and others horseradish, salsa, or marinara sauce.

The Bloody Mary is a great cocktail to experiment with, as the mixers are the stars of this cocktail rather than the spirit. When preparing Bloody Marys, always use the freshest ingredients available.

The Bloody Mary lends itself to a build-your-own setup. Place the vodka, Bloody Mary mix, and different garnishes on your bar and let your guests prepare their own magic. For variety, offer New Orleans garnishes such as medium-sized boiled shrimp, boiled crawfish tails, and strips of crisp bacon. Use your imagination and get creative. You may want to have a contest for the most original Bloody Mary.

SPICE MIX

½ cup black pepper	½ cup Cajun seasoning
½ cup white pepper	¼ cup cayenne pepper
½ cup garlic powder	

Combine all Spice Mix ingredients. Makes 2¼ cups. Will keep in a tightly covered container for up to 6 months. This mix is also good sprinkled on burgers and steaks as they grill.

BLOODY MARY MIX

48 oz. tomato juice	4 oz. catsup
8 oz. Worcestershire sauce	½ cup beet puree
	½ cup celery puree
8 oz. fresh lemon juice	½ cup cucumber puree
2 oz. fresh lime juice	2 tbsp. Spice Mix

Combine all Bloody Mary Mix ingredients and let age overnight for best flavors. Refrigerate until ready to use. Makes about 10 cups.

BLOODY MARY

1¼ oz. vodka
Ice
5-6 oz. Bloody Mary Mix
1 celery stalk
1 lemon wedge
1 lime wedge
Lemon-thyme salt (optional)

Pour vodka into an ice-filled collins glass, and top with Bloody Mary Mix. Stir to blend. Garnish with celery, lemon, and lime. If using a salted rim, first moisten the glass, dip in the salt to coat the rim, carefully fill the glass with ice, and proceed with the recipe, taking care while stirring not to knock off the salt.

BLOODY MARIA

1½ oz. silver tequila
Ice
5-6 oz. Bloody Mary Mix (see recipe above)
1 fresh lime wedge
1 slice jalapeno pepper
Cilantro salt (optional)

Add tequila to an ice-filled collins glass. Add Bloody Mary Mix, and stir to blend. Garnish with lime and jalapeno. If using a salted rim, first moisten the glass, dip in the salt to coat the rim, carefully fill the glass with ice, and proceed with the recipe, taking care while stirring not to knock off the salt.

BLOODY CAESAR

This cocktail is quite popular in the Northeast and especially Canada.

1½ oz. vodka
Ice
4 oz. Bloody Mary Mix (see recipe above)
2 oz. clam juice
1 lime wedge
1 lemon wedge
1 celery stalk

Pour vodka into an ice-filled collins glass. Add Bloody Mary Mix and clam juice. Stir to mix. Garnish with lime, lemon, and celery.

BULL SHOT

1¼ oz. vodka
2 oz. beef broth
2 dashes hot pepper sauce (optional)
Salt and pepper to taste
Ice

Place all ingredients in an ice-filled rocks glass, and stir to mix. Garnish with a small sip straw.

BLOODY BULL

A celery stalk is also a good garnish for this cocktail.

1¼ oz. vodka
3 oz. beef broth
3 oz. Bloody Mary Mix (see recipe above)
Ice
1 lime wedge
1 lemon wedge

Pour all liquids into an ice-filled collins glass. Stir to mix. Garnish with lime and lemon.

RED SNAPPER

1¼ oz. gin
5-6 oz. Bloody Mary Mix (see recipe above)
Ice
1 lime wedge
1 lemon wedge
1 cucumber wheel
Lemon-thyme salt (optional)

Pour liquids into an ice-filled collins glass. Stir to mix. Garnish with lime, lemon, and cucumber. If using a salted rim, first moisten the glass, dip in the salt to coat the rim, carefully fill the glass with ice, and proceed with the recipe, taking care while stirring not to knock off the salt.

COSMONAUT (NONALCOHOLIC)

Here is a nonalcoholic version of the Cosmopolitan for those who, for whatever reason, do not wish to imbibe but want to feel like part of the party.

2 oz. cranberry juice
1 oz. fresh lime juice
½ oz. simple syrup

Ice
½ oz. club soda
1 twist lemon

Pour juices and simple syrup into an ice-filled Boston shaker and shake until well chilled. Strain into a chilled martini glass. Top with club soda. Garnish with lemon.

CHAPTER 13

OCTOBER: ABSINTHE, THE MISUNDERSTOOD SPIRIT

Absinthe is a high-alcohol distilled spirit and one of the most misunderstood spirits of all time. It is also known as the "green fairy," due to its green color. It originated in the late 1700s in Switzerland. In the 1840s, it was given to French soldiers to prevent malaria. They brought their taste for absinthe back with them when they returned to France.

In the late nineteenth century, the bohemian crowd began to favor absinthe over wine. The wine industry was not happy with this, as it was just recovering from a disease epidemic that all but wiped out its grapes. The growers began to push for a ban on the "evil" absinthe. There had been a lot of speculation on the dangers of the spirit. Sometimes absinthe was poisonous, if it was distilled in an inferior way. However, if properly distilled, the spirit was perfectly good and did not cause any more adverse effects than other distilled products.

In August of 1905, a Swiss farmer by the name of Jean Lanfray murdered his family and attempted suicide after consuming absinthe. In fact, he had also drunk numerous glasses of brandy and wine. However, the absinthe took the blame, and by 1914, nearly every country had banned it. The prohibition led to an increase in popularity in France of pastis and, to a lesser extent, ouzo.

Absinthe remained outlawed in the U.S. until 2007, when it was determined that its ingredients were not toxic. Grande wormwood, green anise, and sweet fennel are the main flavoring agents, although there may be more depending on the brand. The ingredients do not contribute to the alcohol content. The alcohol traditionally comes from a redistilled white-grape spirit.

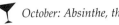

An absinthe fountain is an elaborate contraption that drips ice-cold water from a couple of taps onto sugar cubes that rest in spoons on top of glasses of absinthe. The sweetened water spills into the spirit and transforms it into a cloudy liquid, creating a "louched" absinthe.

Another way to louche absinthe involves a Brouille top, which fits over the glass in place of the spoon. The sugar cube is placed in this top, and ice water is then added. A small hole in the bottom allows the water to seep through to the absinthe.

It is not necessary, however, to own a fountain or Brouille top in order to enjoy absinthe in your home.

ABSINTHE DRIP

Sit back and enjoy this spirit as the French bohemians did in the late 1800s and early 1900s.

1½ oz. absinthe
1 sugar cube
3-4 oz. ice-cold water

Pour absinthe into a rocks glass, and place sugar cube on top of an absinthe spoon. Balance the spoon across the top of the glass and slowly drizzle water over the top of the sugar cube. When the absinthe becomes milky in color, stop adding water. The sugar cube should be dissolved. If not, add to the absinthe and stir with the absinthe spoon to dissolve.

ABSINTHE FRAPPE

6-8 fresh mint leaves
1 oz. absinthe
½ oz. simple syrup
Crushed ice
1 oz. soda water
1 sprig mint

Muddle mint leaves in the bottom of an absinthe glass. Add absinthe and simple syrup, and fill with crushed ice. Pour contents into a Boston shaker and shake vigorously until well chilled and blended. Pour contents back into glass, and top with soda water. Garnish with sprig of mint.

ABSINTHE MARTINI

2 oz. London dry gin
½ oz. dry vermouth
⅛ oz. absinthe
Ice
1 twist lemon

Pour all liquids into an ice-filled Boston shaker and shake until well chilled. Strain into a chilled martini glass. Garnish with lemon.

ABSINTHE FLIP

½ oz. absinthe
½ oz. orange curacao
2 tsp. fresh lemon juice
1 egg white
1 tsp. sugar
Ice
Freshly grated nutmeg

Place liquids and sugar in a Boston shaker and dry shake until well blended and frothy. Add ice and shake again until well chilled. Strain into an absinthe glass and garnish with nutmeg.

ABSINTHE SUISSE

1½ oz. absinthe
½ oz. orange flower water
1 egg white
⅛ oz. light crème de menthe
Ice
1 mint leaf

Pour all liquids into a Boston shaker and dry shake until well blended and frothy. Add ice and shake again until well chilled. Strain into a chilled martini glass, and garnish with mint.

LONDON FAIRY

I created this cocktail for a Gentleman's *Quarterly competition. Even though it did not win, it has been well received. The London Fairy has an interesting combination of flavors that work nicely together. Be careful with the amount of absinthe, so that it does not overpower the cocktail.*

1½ oz. London dry gin
¼ oz. absinthe
1 oz. fresh lime juice
½ oz. pineapple juice
½ oz. simple syrup
1 egg white
Ice
1 fresh pineapple wedge

Pour all liquids into a Boston shaker and dry shake until well blended and frothy. Add ice and shake again until well chilled. Strain into a chilled martini glass and garnish with pineapple.

CORPSE REVIVER #2

This cocktail may also be served up, martini style. The flavors are more intense that way, but I prefer it over ice, which mellows all the flavors as you sip and revive your "corpse." But be careful, as more than two of these in quick succession will ensure that the corpse is permanently done in.

¾ oz. London dry gin
¾ oz. orange curacao
¾ oz. Lillet Blanc or dry vermouth
⅛ oz. absinthe
¾ oz. fresh lemon juice
Ice
1 twist lemon

Build in an ice-filled rocks glass and roll to mix. Garnish with lemon.

MONKEY GLAND

2 oz. London dry gin
¼ oz. absinthe
1½ oz. fresh orange juice
¼ oz. pomegranate syrup or grenadine
Ice
1 orange wedge

Pour all liquids into an ice-filled Boston shaker and shake until well blended and chilled. Strain into a chilled martini glass, and garnish with orange.

CHAPTER 14

NOVEMBER: WHISKEY COCKTAILS

Layered Old Fashioned

"Whiskey" is an umbrella term that covers bourbon, Tennessee whiskey, Irish whiskey, scotch, Canadian whisky, rye, and more. In its most basic form, whiskey is merely beer that has been distilled. No hops are used, but other than that the beginning steps are quite similar. Whiskey is a distilled spirit obtained from the fermented mash of grain, distilled at less than 190 proof, stored in oak barrels, and bottled at a minimum of 40 percent ABV. The oak is important. It imparts its own flavor and, being porous, brings in flavors from the surrounding atmosphere as well.

The spellings *whiskey* and *whisky* are both correct. It just depends on where the spirit is produced. Generally speaking, *whisky* hails from Scotland, England, Wales, Canada, or Japan. Let us now explore some of the different categories.

BOURBON

For a distillate to be called bourbon, the following criteria must be met. The mash must contain at least 51 percent corn (maize) and be distilled to no more than 160 proof (80 percent ABV). No coloring or flavoring may be added. Bourbon must be aged in new, charred, American oak barrels. The distillate must enter the barrels at no more than 125 proof (62.5 percent ABV). Bourbons, like other whiskeys, must be bottled at no less than 80 proof (40 percent ABV). In addition to the above requirements, the distillate must be aged a minimum of two years in order to be called "straight" bourbon. If straight bourbon has been aged less than four years, it must be labeled with the duration of aging of the youngest whiskey in the bottle. Only whiskey produced in the United States may be called bourbon.

TENNESSEE WHISKEY

This is similar to straight bourbon in that the mash is composed of at least 51 percent corn (maize). It is also aged in new, charred, American oak barrels for a minimum of two years. However, most Tennessee distillates undergo the Lincoln County Process, which involves filtration through approximately ten feet of maple charcoal. This step is considered to impart a distinct flavor that is unusually mild. Jack Daniel's and George Dickel are two of the more popular whiskeys that undergo this process. Jack Daniel's original distillery was located in Lincoln County.

IRISH WHISKEY

Irish whiskey is normally distilled three times in pot stills. By law, it must be produced in Ireland and aged in wooden casks for no less than three years.

SCOTCH WHISKY

Scotch whiskies are generally distilled twice. Some are distilled three or more times, even as many as twenty times. Any product labeled *scotch* must be distillated in Scotland with Scottish ingredients and matured a minimum of three years in oak barrels. The age statement on the bottle indicates the youngest whisky in the bottle.

Single-malt whisky is the purebred of scotch, and like a purebred animal, each has its own special personality. Lowland scotches are sweet, Highland ones are smoky, and Islay ones are bold. The single malt is a true treasure.

Like a fine wine, it is made exclusively from a single grain at a single distillery. This does not mean the whisky is from a single batch or single barrel, however. It may be a blend of different barrels but only from that one distillery.

A blended malt whisky combines malt whiskies to produce a specific flavor profile, as determined by the master blender and the proprietary name.

The debate of whether a single malt is better than a blend is a matter of personal preference. I have tasted great examples of both.

CANADIAN WHISKY

By Canadian law, Canadian whiskies must be produced and aged in Canada. They must be distilled from a fermented mash of cereal grains and aged in wood barrels with a capacity level of 700 liters, for not less than three years. The terms "Canadian whisky" and "Canadian rye whisky" are legally indistinguishable in Canada. Canadian whiskies do not require the use of rye or any specific grain in the production process. The predominant grain used is corn (maize). Canadian whiskies may also contain caramel coloring and added flavoring. Also, there is no maximum limit on the alcohol level of the distillate.

AMERICAN RYE WHISKEY

This is made from a mash consisting of at least 51 percent rye; the other ingredients may include corn and malted barley. It is distilled to no more than 160 proof (80 percent ABV). It is to be aged in new, charred, American oak barrels. When the whiskey is put into the barrels, it must be no more than 125 proof (62.5 percent ABV). Rye whiskey that has been aged for at least two years may be designated as "straight" or "straight rye whiskey." This spirit tends to be spicier than its bourbon cousin. Rye is sometimes called the Islay whiskey of America for this reason. Although rye's popularity dwindled to almost nothing after Prohibition, more and more bartenders and consumers are using it in classics such as the Manhattan and Old Fashioned.

SOUTHERN COMFORT

This American spirit was concocted by a New Orleans bartender named Martin Wilkes Heron, in the late 1800s. Its secret blend of ingredients includes peach juice. Southern Comfort may substituted for bourbon in cocktails, but remember that Southern Comfort is much sweeter. Be sure to adjust your sweetening ingredients to accommodate this.

CORN WHISKEY (MOONSHINE)

Also known as "corn liquor," "white dog," or "white lightning," this American spirit is made from a mash of at least 80 percent corn. The recipe is based on the old illegal moonshine, except corn whiskey is aged. Unlike bourbon, it may be aged in used or uncharred barrels. The aging is usually brief—six months or less—during which time the whiskey absorbs the flavors and color of the barrels and any off flavors are greatly reduced.

APPLEJACK

Applejack was originally produced by concentrating cider either by freeze distillation ("jacking") or evaporation distillation. Laird & Company, located in Scobeyville, New Jersey, is the oldest licensed applejack distiller in the United States. During the American Revolution, George Washington asked Robert Laird for his recipe.

MANHATTAN DRY

The history of the Manhattan cocktail, like so many others, is up for discussion and debate, as there are many different stories of its origin. One was that it was created at the Manhattan Club for Lady Randolph Churchill (nee Jennie Jerome) in 1874. This is likely not true, because she was in France and pregnant with Winston at the time. The Manhattan was mentioned in the Democrat *newspaper in 1882 and in* Valentine's Manual of New York, *published in 1923, which attributed it to Mr. Black, a bartender on Broadway in the 1860s. In any case, it has stood the test of time and become one of the great classic cocktails, and it is gaining in popularity again.*

2 oz. bourbon or rye
1 oz. dry vermouth
Ice
2-3 drops Angostura bitters
1 twist lemon

Place all liquids in an ice-filled Boston shaker and stir until well chilled. Strain into a chilled martini glass and garnish with lemon.

MANHATTAN SWEET

2 oz. bourbon or rye
1 oz. sweet vermouth
2-3 drops Angostura bitters
Ice
1 maraschino cherry

Place all liquids in an ice-filled Boston shaker and stir until well chilled. Strain into a chilled martini glass and garnish with cherry.

MANHATTAN PERFECT

2 oz. bourbon or rye
½ oz. sweet vermouth
½ oz. dry vermouth
2-3 drops Angostura bitters
Ice
1 maraschino cherry

Place all liquids in an ice-filled Boston shaker and stir until well chilled. Strain into a chilled martini glass and garnish with cherry.

MILLIONAIRE COCKTAIL

This may not make you a real millionaire, but after drinking a couple, you sure will feel like one. Sit back, enjoy, and think of the good life.

2 oz. rye
1 oz. orange curacao
1 oz. pomegranate syrup or grenadine
1 tsp. raspberry liqueur
1 egg white
Ice
1 orange wheel

Pour all liquids into a Boston shaker and dry shake until well blended and frothy. Add ice and shake again until well chilled. Strain into a chilled martini glass and garnish with orange.

KENTUCKY SUNSHINE

I created this cocktail for the tenth-anniversary radio show of "Chef and the Fatman." It is similar to a whiskey sour but with the addition of egg white and Aztec chocolate bitters.

  2 oz. bourbon
  1 oz. fresh lemon juice
  ½ oz. agave nectar (or to taste depending on
     tartness of lemon)
  1 egg white
  3-4 drops Fee Brothers Aztec chocolate bitters
  Ice
  1 lemon wheel

Pour all liquids into a Boston shaker and dry shake until well blended and frothy. Add ice and shake again until well chilled. Strain into a chilled martini glass and garnish with lemon.

OLD FASHIONED (CLASSIC VERSION)

  Ice cubes
  2 oz. bourbon or rye
  ¼ oz. simple syrup
  3 dashes Angostura bitters
  1 twist orange or lemon

Place 2 ice cubes in a rocks glass. Add liquids and stir. Add 2 more ice cubes and stir again. While stirring, add more ice, until glass is full. Garnish with orange or lemon.

OLD FASHIONED (AMERICAN VERSION)

1 orange slice	3 dashes Angostura bitters
1 maraschino cherry	Ice
¼ oz. simple syrup	2 oz. bourbon or rye

Place fruit, simple syrup, and bitters in a rocks glass and muddle to release the juices. Fill glass with ice. Add whiskey and stir to blend.

OTONO EN ESPANA (AUTUMN IN SPAIN)

Yours truly created this for the Cocktails and Curds event in New Orleans, sponsored by the St. James Cheese Company. The cocktail was well received and was paired with a Spanish Manchego cheese. This cocktail is a great accompaniment for a fruit-and-cheese platter, especially one with fall fruits such as pear and some flavorful cheeses.

1¼ oz. Irish whiskey	3 oz. ginger beer
½ oz. pear liqueur	Ice
1 tbsp. fig preserves	2-3 dashes walnut bitters
¼ oz. fresh lemon juice	1 cube fresh pear

Place whiskey, liqueur, preserves, lemon juice, and bitters in an-ice filled Boston shaker and shake to mix and chill. Double strain into an ice-filled collins glass and top with ginger beer. Garnish with pear.

GMNO DAISY

I created this cocktail and presented it on air for WGNO's "Good Morning New Orleans" (GMNO) anniversary show. If satsumas are not available, mandarin orange juice makes a great substitute.

1½ oz. rye	Ice
½ oz. orange curacao	2 oz. club soda
2 oz. satsuma juice	1 satsuma wheel
¼ oz. agave nectar	

Pour whiskey, orange curacao, satsuma juice, and agave nectar into an ice-filled collins glass. Roll into a Boston shaker to blend. Top with club soda. Garnish with satsuma.

ROB ROY

This is basically a Manhattan made with scotch. The variety of scotch you choose will determine whether the cocktail has a light or heavy peat flavor. Experiment with different brands to find the one that is right for you and your guests.

2 oz. scotch
1 oz. sweet vermouth
2-3 dashes Angostura bitters
Ice
1 maraschino cherry

Pour all liquids into an ice-filled Boston shaker and shake until well chilled. Strain into a chilled martini glass and garnish with cherry.

SCOFFLAW

The term "scofflaw" was born during Prohibition, when the Boston Herald *held a competition for readers to come up with a new word for "a lawless drinker of illegally made or illegally obtained liquor." Two winners, from 25,000 entries, shared the $200 prize. The Scofflaw cocktail was created at Harry's Bar in Paris.*

2 oz. bourbon
2 oz. dry vermouth
½ oz. fresh lemon juice
¼ oz. grenadine

1 dash orange bitters
Ice
1 twist lemon

Pour all liquids into an ice-filled Boston shaker and shake until well blended and chilled. Strain into a chilled martini glass, and garnish with lemon.

BLUE BLAZER

This was created by "Professor" Jerry Thomas, author of the first book on bartending. He liked to travel the country and ply his trade and showmanship at various bars. Please use caution when preparing this flaming cocktail. It is best to practice with just liquid to learn the pouring technique. You must first start with two silver or other heat-resistant mugs. Place about 2 oz. water in each and pour it back and forth between the mugs, extending the distance with each pour. After you have mastered the technique with water, practice with hot water, making sure you don't spill any either on the floor or yourself. Only then are you ready to graduate to preparing the Blue Blazer.

Boiling water
2 oz. scotch
1 tsp. powdered sugar

Heat your mugs with boiling water and throw out the water. Add scotch to 1 mug and 2 oz. boiling water to the other. Light the scotch with a long match and start tossing the liquids back and forth between the mugs, creating a blue stream of flame. Use extreme caution when doing this. Make sure your guests stand back so they are not accidentally burned. Once you have gone back and forth between the mugs 2-3 times, extinguish the flame by placing 1 mug over the other. Pour into a rocks glass that has a spoon in it, which will help prevent the glass from cracking when the boiling liquid is poured in. Stir in the sugar to sweeten.

WARD 8

There are many variations of this cocktail, but I think this one is the best. The Ward 8 was created in Boston in 1898 to honor the election of Martin M. Lomasney to the state legislature.

2 oz. rye or scotch   1 tsp. grenadine
½ oz. fresh lemon juice   Ice
½ oz. fresh orange   1 maraschino cherry
  juice

Pour all the liquids into an ice-filled Boston shaker and shake to chill. Strain into a chilled martini glass and garnish with cherry.

GODFATHER

This cocktail is feisty. To make a Godmother, which is sweet with a kick, just substitute vodka for the scotch. We need both a godfather and godmother, and these are equally tasty.

1 oz. scotch	Ice
1 oz. amaretto	

Pour liquids into an ice-filled Boston shaker and shake to chill. Strain into an ice-filled rocks glass.

BOBBY BURNS

As a tribute to the poet Robert Burns, serve this with Scottish shortbread.

2 oz. scotch	½ oz. Benedictine
1 oz. sweet vermouth	Ice

Pour all liquids into an ice-filled Boston shaker and shake until well chilled. Stain into a chilled martini glass.

BOULEVARDIER COCKTAIL

This is a rye variation of the classic negroni.

1 oz. rye	Ice
1 oz. Campari	1 twist orange
1 oz. sweet vermouth	

Pour all liquids into an ice-filled Boston shaker and

shake until well chilled. Strain into a chilled martini glass and garnish with orange.

PRAIRIE OYSTER

This cocktail is not for the faint of heart and best drunk in one gulp. It is reputed to cure a hangover.

1 egg yolk
1 oz. bourbon
2 dashes hot pepper sauce
2 dashes Worcestershire sauce
2 dashes fresh lemon juice

Place egg yolk in the bottom of a small rocks glass. Add bourbon and then the remaining ingredients.

RHETT BUTLER

This cocktail and the next honor a memorable fictional Southern couple. But beware. Although these cocktails may seem sweet, they are just as feisty as their namesakes.

1½ oz. Southern Comfort
¼ oz. fresh lime juice
¼ oz. fresh lemon juice
½ oz. orange curacao
Ice
1 lime wedge

Pour all liquids into an ice-filled Boston shaker and shake until well chilled and blended. Strain into a chilled martini glass, and garnish with lime.

SCARLETT O'HARA

1¼ oz. Southern Comfort
1 oz. cranberry juice
¼ oz. fresh lime juice
2-3 drops vanilla bitters
Ice
1 lime wedge

Pour all liquids into an ice-filled Boston shaker and shake until well chilled and blended. Strain into a chilled martini glass, and garnish with lime.

PRESBYTERIAN

2 oz. blended malt whiskey or bourbon
2 oz. club soda
2 oz. ginger ale or lemon-lime soda
Ice
1 twist lemon

Pour all liquids into an ice-filled rocks glass, and garnish with lemon.

THE ALGONQUIN COCKTAIL

This cocktail is named for the Algonquin Hotel in New York, which played host to many of the literary elite. It is one of three Literary Landmark Hotels in the United States, along with the Hotel Monteleone in New Orleans and the Plaza in New York.

1½ oz. rye
¾ oz. dry vermouth
¾ oz. pineapple juice
Ice

Pour all liquids into an ice-filled Boston shaker and shake until well chilled. Strain into a chilled martini glass. No garnish necessary.

MAMIE TAYLOR

This cocktail, which has all but been forgotten, was named after a Broadway actress who was on the stage in the late nineteenth and early twentieth centuries.

2 oz. scotch   Ice
¾ oz. fresh lime juice   1 lime wedge
4 oz. ginger beer

Build in an ice-filled rocks glass, stir to mix, and garnish with lime.

BLOOD AND SAND

This cocktail was named after a Rudolph Valentino bullfighter movie. The combination of ingredients may not seem particularly appetizing, but when prepared properly, a Blood and Sand is a real taste treat.

1 oz. scotch   ¾ oz. sweet vermouth
1 oz. fresh orange juice   Ice
¾ oz. cherry brandy   1 maraschino cherry

Pour all liquids into an ice-filled Boston shaker and shake until well chilled. Strain into a chilled martini glass. Garnish with cherry.

SEELBACH COCKTAIL

This cocktail is named for the Seelbach Hotel in Louisville, Kentucky and was first prepared around 1917. The recipe was lost until 1995. The Seelbach is an interesting twist on the classic Champagne Cocktail.

1 oz. bourbon
½ oz. Cointreau
4 dashes Angostura bitters
4 dashes Peychaud's bitters

Ice
5 oz. Champagne or sparkling wine
1 twist orange

Place bourbon, Cointreau, and bitters in an ice-filled Boston shaker and shake to mix. Strain into a Champagne flute, and top with Champagne or sparkling wine. Garnish with orange.

LEATHERNECK COCKTAIL

This cocktail bears the slang name of the U.S. Marine Corps.

2 oz. blended Canadian whisky
¾ oz. blue curacao
½ oz. fresh lime juice
Ice
1 lime wheel

Pour all liquids into an ice-filled Boston shaker and shake to blend and chill. Strain into a chilled martini glass. Garnish with lime.

CHAPTER 15

DECEMBER: HOLIDAY COCKTAILS

Wassail Bowl

December is usually busy with people making holiday preparations and hosting and attending parties at home and work. Yet it is a festive time that calls for something extra special. These cocktails may take a little time to prepare but will awe your guests. There are recipes that may be made in advance and in quantity, so that your guests may help themselves with little fuss and you can still be the star for your great cocktails.

December 5 is the anniversary of the repeal of the Volstead Act in 1933, which ended that dark period of the American cocktail, Prohibition. This chapter concludes with a tribute to that momentous occasion. Start your celebration with some nonalcoholic libations, and then raise a toast with the real thing.

WASSAIL BOWL

This is a traditional English holiday beverage. It was first made in that country's cider-producing areas. "Wassail" refers to the ceremony of singing and drinking to the health of the apple trees and to ward off evil spirits. It began as a toast, waes hael. *Revelers may have held up cups of spiced cider as they greeted friends and neighbors. Over time, "wassail" became less of a greeting and more often referred to the drink.*

A traditional Wassail Bowl was a hot beverage prepared with hard cider, cinnamon, sugar, and nutmeg and topped with spiced toast (hence the term "toast" when raising a glass). The modern recipe often begins with a red wine, fruit juice, and mulled ale, and occasionally brandy or sherry will be added. Then sliced apples, oranges, lemons, and pineapple, as well as cinnamon sticks and sugar, are added for flavor. This mixture is heated, and a great aroma fills the house. The Wassail is then ladled into punch cups.

A tasty Wassail Bowl recipe follows. Don't be afraid to experiment, but always keep the hard cider as your base.

2 qt. hard cider	1 tsp. allspice
½ cup brandy	6 whole cloves
½ cup sherry	1 medium orange, sliced
1 cup sugar	1 lemon, sliced
3 cinnamon sticks	1 fresh apple, sliced

Place all ingredients except fruit in a heat-resistant pot. A slow cooker works great, as it gently heats the liquid and stews the spices. When warmed, transfer to a heat-resistant punchbowl and add fruit. To be really traditional, add bits of spiced toast to your punch cup, and toast friends and family. Makes about 6 8-oz. cups.

FREDA KAUFFMAN'S EGGNOG

Eggnog is another traditional holiday beverage. Its roots are quite murky. Some say that eggnog derived from the various milk-and-wine punches of Europe and was brought to colonial America. However, the colonies put their own twist on it by using the more available rum instead of wine. This was called "egg and grog," which was shortened to "egg 'n' grog" and then "eggnog." There is also a theory that eggnog started out as a mixture of Spanish sherry and milk that was served in a carved wooden mug known as a "noggin." This was called "egg and grog in a noggin" and was shortened to "eggnog." In any case, eggnog has become a traditional beverage from late November through December. It is a rich, creamy, spicy treat that may be served either cold or warm. Below is one of my favorite recipes. I first had eggnog when I was quite young, and this is what my grandmother, Freda Kauffman, served. It is a lot of work and a bit time consuming, but the results are great.

12 eggs	1 tsp. freshly grated nutmeg
1 cup sugar	1 tsp. cinnamon
2 qt. whole milk	1 tbsp. vanilla extract
1 qt. half-and-half	1 qt. French vanilla ice
1 qt. heavy cream	cream
2 cups bourbon or	Cinnamon and nutmeg
rum	for garnish

Separate the eggs and set the whites aside. Beat the yolks with the sugar until lemon colored and sugar is completely dissolved. Gently heat the mixture with milk until slightly thickened. Set aside to cool to room temperature.

Meanwhile, beat the egg whites until stiff peaks form.

Place yolk mixture in a large punchbowl and gradually add half-and-half, cream, bourbon or rum, nutmeg, cinnamon, and vanilla extract. Once well mixed, taste and add more spices if needed. Place about ⅓ of the egg whites in the eggnog and gently fold in, trying not to deflate them. Continue to add the egg whites until all are blended in.

Just before serving, add scoops of ice cream and dust the top with cinnamon and nutmeg. Ladle into punch cups and enjoy. Makes about 24 8-oz. cups.

WHITE RUSSIAN

Use vanilla vodka or add vanilla bitters for a nice variation on this classic.

1¼ oz. vodka   1 oz. half-and-half
1 oz. Kahlua   Ice

Build in an ice-filled rocks glass and roll in Boston shaker to blend. Garnish with a sip straw.

BLACK RUSSIAN

1¼ oz. vodka
1¼ oz. Kahlua
Ice

Build in an ice-filled rocks glass, stir briefly to blend, and garnish with a sip straw.

COLORADO BULLDOG

1¼ oz. vodka	Ice
1 oz. Kahlua	1 oz. cola
2 oz. half-and-half	

Pour vodka, Kahlua, and half-and-half into an ice-filled collins glass, and roll to blend. Top with cola. No garnish needed.

BRANDY MILK PUNCH

This New Orleans brunch tradition is not a bad way to get your calcium. For a variation, substitute bourbon or rum for the brandy. Either one works well, so experiment and decide which you prefer.

1¼ oz. brandy	2 oz. half-and-half
½ oz. simple syrup or to taste	Ice
	Freshly grated nutmeg
1 tsp. vanilla extract	

Build in an ice-filled Boston shaker and shake to blend. Strain into an ice-filled collins glass, and garnish with nutmeg.

TOASTED ALMOND

1½ oz. coffee liqueur	Ice
1½ oz. Amaretto	Grated chocolate
2 oz. half-and-half	

Build in an ice-filled rocks glass, roll to mix, and garnish with chocolate.

MUDSLIDE

This cocktail is also good using hot coffee in place of the half-and-half and topped with sweetened whipped cream.

1 oz. vodka	3 oz. half-and-half
1 oz. Irish cream liqueur	Ice
1 oz. Amaretto	Grated chocolate

Pour all liquids into an ice-filled Boston shaker and shake until well blended and chilled. Strain into an ice-filled rocks glass, and garnish with chocolate.

BUSHWHACKER

This cocktail has many variations. This is my favorite.

1½ oz. coffee liqueur
¾ oz. light rum
½ oz. light crème de cacao
1½ oz. coconut cream
2 oz. half-and-half
Ice
1 cherry

Pour all liquids into an ice-filled Boston shaker and shake until well chilled and blended. Strain into a tall glass filled with crushed ice. Garnish with cherry and a large straw.

HOLIDAY COCKTAIL

This twist on the classic Brandy Milk Punch features some great holiday flavors.

    1 oz. Drambuie
    ½ oz. scotch
    3-4 dashes chocolate bitters
    1 tsp. vanilla extract or 3-4 drops vanilla bitters
    4-5 oz. half-and-half
    Ice
    Freshly grated nutmeg

Pour all liquids into an ice-filled Boson shaker and shake until well blended and chilled. Strain into an ice-filled rocks glass and garnish with a dusting of nutmeg.

SMOKIN' BROTHER

This is a great way to relax after a cold and hectic day of shopping or putting up Christmas decorations.

    Ice
    ¼ oz. scotch (preferably an Islay)
    1¼ oz. Benedictine
    ¼ oz. Domaine de Canton
    ½ oz. rye
    3-4 drops orange bitters

Fill a rocks glass with ice, add the scotch, and set aside. Place remaining ingredients in an ice-filled Boston shaker and shake to chill. Empty the rocks glass and strain the contents of the Boston shaker into the scotch-coated glass. (Just a thought, but you may want to consume the scotch rather than discard it. I consider it alcohol abuse to waste good scotch.)

PERUVIAN CHRISTMAS

I created this cocktail, and it was included in a New Orleans Times-Picayune *article in 2010.*

1½ oz. pisco
¼ oz. maraschino liqueur
½ oz. Amaretto
1 oz. fresh lemon juice
½ oz. agave nectar
3-4 dashes Peychaud's bitters
Ice
1 maraschino cherry

Pour all liquids into an ice-filled Boston shaker and shake until well chilled. Strain into a chilled martini glass. Drop cherry into the glass.

HOT BUTTERED RUM

This beverage is traditionally prepared with hot water, but hot milk makes it richer and creamier. The Spiced Butter Mix also makes a great spread for your toast or biscuit in the morning.

SPICED BUTTER MIX

> 1 stick unsalted butter
> ¼ tsp. cinnamon
> ¼ tsp. freshly grated nutmeg
> ¼ tsp. allspice
> ½ tsp. brown sugar

HOT BUTTERED RUM

> 1 tbsp. Spiced Butter Mix
> 1¼ oz. gold rum
> 5 oz. hot water or hot milk
> Freshly grated nutmeg or 1 cinnamon stick

Place Spiced Butter Mix ingredients in a bowl and blend. Refrigerate, covered, until needed. Makes enough mix for approximately 8 servings.

Heat a coffee mug with hot water and discard water. Add Spiced Butter Mix to hot mug. Add rum and top with hot water or hot milk. Garnish with nutmeg or cinnamon.

TOM AND JERRY

As tasty as the batter is, you probably will not have any

leftovers. *This cocktail will definitely warm you up after a day out in the December weather.*

TOM AND JERRY BATTER

6 eggs, separated
¼ cup superfine or granulated sugar (superfine dissolves easier)
1 tsp. vanilla extract
1 cup powdered milk

To make the batter, beat the egg yolks in a small bowl until light and frothy; set aside. In another bowl, beat egg whites, sugar, and vanilla until stiff peaks form. Slowly fold in the yolks, taking care to keep the mixture fluffy. Gradually add powdered milk. Batter will keep in refrigerator for about 1 week. If it separates, just whip carefully with a wire whisk before using.

TOM AND JERRY

3 tbsp. Tom and Jerry Batter or to taste
1¼ oz. brandy, rum, or bourbon
6 oz. boiling water
Freshly grated nutmeg

To make the cocktail, place 3 tbsp. Tom and Jerry Batter in an 8-oz. coffee mug. Add spirit of choice, and stir to blend. While stirring, pour in hot water to top of mug. Garnish with nutmeg.

TRIBUTE TO THE REPEAL OF PROHIBITION

December 5 is the anniversary of the end of Prohibition, so it's a great day to celebrate the cocktail. To do it properly, start with a couple of the nonalcoholic libations below, and then at your chosen hour (midnight or sooner), begin sipping the alcoholic ones.

GINGER BEER PUNCH (NONALCOHOLIC)

Both this punch and the following one are alcohol free, but they are also quite tasty if you choose to add either gold rum or bourbon.

2 cups fresh-brewed black tea, room temperature
1 cup superfine or granulated sugar
1½ cups fresh orange juice
½ cup fresh lemon juice
24 oz. ginger beer or ginger ale
Orange slices
Lemon slices

Pour tea into a large punch bowl. Stir in sugar until dissolved. Add juices. Refrigerate until well chilled.

Add ginger beer. Garnish with fruit slices floating on top. Makes about 8 8-oz. cups.

GINGER–APPLE PUNCH (NONALCOHOLIC)

1 cup apple juice
Juice of 1 lime
2 tbsp. simple syrup (more if a sweeter punch is
    desired)
24 oz. ginger beer
Fresh apple slices

Pour all liquids into a punch bowl and stir to mix. Garnish with apples. Makes about 4 8-oz. cups.

THREE–MILE–LIMIT COCKTAIL

This cocktail was invented at Harry's Bar in Paris. At the time, due to Prohibition in the U.S., you could not even legally imbibe alcohol at sea, unless you were at least three miles from the coast. This is a rather unusual tasting cocktail. I much prefer its cousin, the Twelve-Mile Limit. But either one is a great way to celebrate the end of Prohibition.

1 oz. brandy
½ oz. light rum
¼ oz. grenadine or pomegranate syrup
¼ oz. fresh lemon juice
Ice

Pour all liquids into an ice-filled Boston shaker and shake until well chilled and blended. Strain into a chilled martini glass.

TWELVE–MILE–LIMIT COCKTAIL

At one time Prohibition laws even required that a boat be at least twelve miles off the coast in order to serve alcohol.

1 oz. light rum
½ oz. rye
½ oz. brandy
½ oz. grenadine
½ oz. fresh lemon juice
Ice
1 twist lemon

Pour all liquids into an ice-filled Boston shaker and shake until well chilled. Strain into a chilled martini glass and garnish with lemon.

BEE'S KNEES

This cocktail was a great way to mask the strong alcoholic taste of the bathtub gin that was available during Prohibition. It was common at the time to say that something good was "the bee's knees." To make the honey syrup, mix equal parts honey and hot water.

1½ oz. gin
¼ oz. honey syrup, room temperature
1 tsp. fresh lemon juice
Ice
1 twist lemon

Pour all liquids into an ice-filled Boston shaker and shake until well blended. Strain into a chilled martini glass. Garnish with lemon.

HOT TODDY

This beverage helps soothe a sore throat or warms you up when you come in from outside. It is very good as a nightcap on a chilly winter's night.

> Boiling water
> 1¼ oz. bourbon
> ¼ oz. honey or agave nectar
> ¼ oz. fresh lemon juice
> 5 oz. hot water or hot tea

Heat an Irish coffee mug by adding boiling water and letting sit for 10-15 seconds. Dump out water and add bourbon, honey or agave nectar, and lemon juice. Stir to blend and top with hot water or hot tea.

PINK SQUIRREL (CLASSIC)

> 1½ oz. crème de noyaux (almond liqueur)
> 1¼ oz. light crème de cacao
> 2 oz. half-and-half
> Ice

Pour all liquids into an ice-filled Boston shaker and shake until well blended and frothy. Strain into a chilled martini glass. May also be served on the rocks.

PINK SQUIRREL (NOUVEAU)

1½ oz. Amaretto
1¼ oz. crème de cacao
2 oz. half-and-half
¼ oz. grenadine
Ice

Pour all liquids into an ice-filled Boston shaker and shake until well blended and frothy. Strain into a chilled martini glass. May also be served on the rocks.

ORANGE DREAM

This is a very good cocktail after dinner or as a nightcap to ensure sweet dreams.

1 oz. Grand Marnier
½ oz. Amaretto
¼ oz. light crème de cacao
Ice
1 oz. sweetened whipped cream
Orange zest

Place spirits in an ice-filled Boston shaker, and shake until well chilled. Strain into a martini glass and float the cream on top. Garnish by grating some orange zest on top of the cream.

THE LAST WORD

In any situation, there is always someone who has the last word. Let us end our brief journey through the world of spirits with a cocktail that is aptly named "The Last Word." Created at the Detroit Athletic Club in the 1930s, this once-forgotten cocktail is regaining popularity.

1 oz. London dry gin
1 oz. green chartreuse
1 oz. maraschino liqueur
1 oz. fresh lime juice
Ice
1 lime wedge

Pour all ingredients into an ice-filled Boston shaker and shake until well chilled. Strain into a chilled martini glass, and garnish with lime.

So ends our journey together, but yours is by no means complete. Hopefully, this book has piqued your interest not only in cocktail making but in tasting and getting to know the various spirits that are available.

While a professional bartender may need to strictly follow standardized recipes in a particular establishment, you should view cocktail recipes as templates, not a set of hard-and-fast rules. Always keep in mind that experimentation is fun, and if you like the taste, it is good.

FURTHER READING

Abou-Ganim, Tony. *Vodka Distilled*. (Surrey Books)

Arthur, Stanley Clisby. *Famous New Orleans Drinks and How to Mix 'Em*. (Pelican)

Blue, Anthony Dias. *The Complete Book of Spirits*. (HarperCollins)

Boothby, Wm. (Cocktail). *The World's Drinks and How to Mix Them*. (Mud Puddle Books)

Conrad, Barnaby, III. *Absinthe: History in a Bottle*. (Chronicle Books)

DeGroff, Dale. *The Art of the Cocktail*. (Clarkson Potter)

———. *The Essential Cocktail*. (Clarkson Potter)

Delahaye, Marie-Claude. *Absinthe: The Living Legend*. (Equinox)

Difford, Simon. *Difford's Encyclopedia of Cocktails*. (Firefly Books)

Domine, Andre. *The Ultimate Guide to Spirits and Cocktails*. (Ullmann)

Embry, David A. *The Fine Art of Mixing Drinks*. (Mud Puddle Books)

Haigh, Ted. *Vintage Spirits and Cocktails*. (Quarry Books)

Harrington, Paul, and Laura Moorhead. *Cocktail: The Drinks Bible for the 21st Century*. (Viking)

Katsigris, Costas, and Chris Thomas. *The Bar and Beverage Book*. (John Wiley and Sons)

Lawlon, C. F. *The Mixologist*. (Mud Puddle Books)

Meier, Frank. *The Artistry of Mixing Drinks*. (Mud Puddle Books)

Miller, Anistatia, and Jared Brown. *Spiritous Journey: A History of Drinks.* (Mixellany Limited)
The Savoy Cocktail Book. (Pavilion Books)
Wondrich, David. *Imbibe!* (Penguin)

INDEX